IN AWE IN ARGENTINA

ROCKY GRAMS

CREATION HOUSE
A STRANG COMPANY

IN AWE IN ARGENTINA by Rocky Grams
Published by Creation House
A Strang Company
600 Rinehart Road
Lake Mary, Florida 32746
www.creationhouse.com

Unless otherwise noted, all Scripture quotations are from the King James Version.

Scripture quotations marked NKJV are from the New King James Version of the Bible. Copyright © 1979, 1980, 1982 by Thomas Nelson, Inc., publishers. Used by permission.

Scripture quotations marked NIV are from the Holy Bible, New International Version. Copyright © 1973, 1978, 1984, International Bible Society. Used by permission.

Cover design by Terry Clifton

Library of Congress Control Number: 2006926085
International Standard Book Number-10: 1-59979-022-X
International Standard Book Number-13: 978-1-59979-022-0

First Edition

06 07 08 09 10 — 987654321
Printed in the United States of America

This is a book for those people that have been touched by God, and have not realized that the simple touch had the purpose of awakening a deep and desperate hunger inside to know Him more.

Rocky and Sherry Grams have marked my life and that of Alejandra, my wife. They have become true pastors for us in the stage of our preparation as future leaders. We will always be eternally grateful to them.

They have had the opportunity to live intensely the decades in which God has visited Argentina, and they have been wholly dedicated to the development of the leaders that the revival would need.

If you desire more of God, you will be trapped by the pages of this sensational book.

—Pastor Osvaldo Carnível
Catedral de la Fe, Buenos Aires
Host of Spanish 700 Club

It was a freezing morning of a crude winter when I came across Rocky for the first time. The cold seemed to stick between one's bones and filter into the soul. Having been invited to share breakfast with one of the professors of the Bible Institute, I sat down at the table and in front of a steaming pot of coffee. Soon he appeared with his characteristic open smile. He offered a general greeting and then stopped at the squalid figure that I presented at that time. "Dante Gebel," he said to my amazement, "welcome, man of God, chosen of the Father."

I could barely respond. The man had choked me with praises that truly were grandiloquent and undeserved.

Then, taking his breakfast cup he looked me in the eyes once again and pronounced: "We value the fact that you are here. Thanks for serving. Your surrender is evident."

I was there in a circumstantial way. I didn't even work for him, and we had just become acquainted. But he already knew my name. Someone had filled him in on who this intruder was and what is better yet: he had poked around in my heart; he dove into my soul in those few seconds that it had taken him to be seated at the table. That is the best biographical sketch of Rocky Grams. Anecdotes like this one define him wholly.

As the years have gone by, I have learned that these small and invaluable attitudes are the ones that have marked thousands of the servants of God that have passed through the life of the prestigious Bible Institute, which has the good fortune to have Grams at the helm. Each alumnus with whom I have spoken agrees with the same common denominator: the life and timely words of Rocky that have lived beyond any theological subject, any spiritual experience they may have lived. My own wife, who was part of the army of the institute, remembers those small details over any brilliant exposition in any of his classrooms.

That is why when I found out that he was writing this book, in some way, I knew that divine justice was being carried out. Only a shrewd observer who lives watching for those small details that set a person apart is capable of relating the history of a nation touched by the Lord, with a criterion that transforms it into a unique book. Maybe because revivals, though they are generated by God, materialize through persons He has chosen. And Rocky is not just a simple narrator of chronicles that passes through the story without stopping to see each person. A man who can take time in the hurry and scurry of everyday life to learn the name of each student and get to know their dreams is someone who values the man over the gift, and that transforms him as an author to be more than qualified to speak of the move of God in our country.

Rocky does not take a photograph of the beach and then compile postcards in a book; he possesses the gift of lingering with each grain of sand, no matter how insignificant it may appear to the trivial look of any mortal.

In Awe in Argentina has a guiding thread, almost invisible to coarse eyes, but perceptible for those that beyond the book, perceive the essence. Precisely this is a work that pauses to see the instruments of the Lord. Instead of constructing a tabernacle around a spiritual experience and trying to squeeze a theological thesis out of the supernatural, Rocky determines a marked emphasis on the men and women that were in the eye of the divine hurricane, at the right moment.

He speaks of them and of each one with a surety of one who has seen them develop, grow, and mature.

Rocky was part of the majority of those dreams that later would be turned into sources of revival. He was with them; he lived with their doubts and with their successes. He fought against their youthful errors and helped them walk on turbulent waters. But he also dove to the depths of their souls.

As an author, Rocky knows the waterfalls and the edges of the terrain on which he moves, and he does it in a totally natural way. He tries not to be bombastic and limits himself to the facts, just as they occurred. This is the chronicle of a traveler who walks through the revival, the diary of the exodus of someone who has seen dozens of servants of God grow who now surprise the whole world. I am sure that this exhaustive work will become a part of the archives of the larger history of the move of God in the world and with the passing of the decades will be resource material for thousands of visionaries that yearn to live something similar. "God wants His river to flow through the whole world," says the author. "May He find us faithful so that we may participate according to the parameters of His will. He is giving dreams and visions right now and wants each one of us to be involved."

In short, *In Awe in Argentina* is an authentic work, brilliant and sharply focused on those small details that may be passed over by any observer, but not by Grams. Don't be confused, this is not a book that catalogues or a simple chronology of the events that have moved a nation. This is an authentic dossier of an open heart, a manual that all Christians should read at some time. And if that were not enough, it is written by one of the few men who possess the enormous ability to pause and notice the small, the invisible, that which others would pass over. I always held to the idea that only someone who could handle an enormous power of synthesis, a fluid sense of the opportunity and above all, a great spiritual sensitivity, is capable of marking a man with just four words: "Your surrender is evident."

—DANTE GEBEL
EVANGELIST

One of the things my wife and I looked forward to during my time as Malaysia's ambassador to Argentina (1996–1999) was spending time with Rocky and Sherry Grams. Their faith and passion inspired us onward and upward. I am so glad and excited that the Lord has now laid it upon Rocky's heart to finally write this book—now everyone can sit with Rocky and be ministered to.

To meet Rocky Grams and to hear his awesome accounts of the work of the Holy Spirit in Argentina is to walk into the Book of Acts! There are few as qualified to talk about the Argentine revival, and offer lessons and insights into it, as he. Under the anointing of the Holy Spirit, he has helped chronicle it, fuel it, and sustain it in the hundreds of pastors, evangelists, and church leaders who have graduated from the River Plate Bible College.

In Awe in Argentina is really a template for what the modern church should look like. It will open your eyes to the reality of the living God. It will inspire and encourage you. It will birth in you fresh faith to believe God for great things wherever you are. It is tonic to the tired and the weary and fresh bread for the hungry. It will be hard to settle for anything less after this!

—DENNIS IGNATIUS
AMBASSADOR TO CANADA
FORMER AMBASSADOR OF MALAYSIA TO ARGENTINA
AUTHOR OF FIRE BEGETS FIRE (www.firebegetsfire.org)

When it comes to reading a book, the best thing is to know the author! I have been in Argentina on several occasions and observed firsthand the ministry and even more, the acceptance and authority of Rocky and Sherry Grams with the people and spiritual leaders of that nation. They were in Argentina when "the tide was out" and they continued to believe that God had promised a move of His Spirit in that land. *In Awe in Argentina* documents the answer to that belief. They had participated in training many of the young people who now lead this incredible move of God. It is one thing to observe in a detached manner and report "objectively" what is seen. It is another to report with breathless enthusiasm and to document through personal participation what God is doing. That is the Bible way. Read to be encouraged, read to believe that when the tide is out it is the time to teach, and prepare for the rush of God's answering waves of revival!

—RICK HOWARD
BIBLE TEACHER AND SPEAKER
AUTHOR OF *THE JUDGMENT SEAT OF CHRIST*, *THE KING DESCRIBES HIS KINGDOM*, *RESTORING RESTORERS*, AND *STRATEGY FOR TRIUMPH*

Author Rocky Grams' unique role as observer, participant, facilitator, and now recorder of one of recent history's more fascinating and ongoing spiritual renewals allows the reader glimpses through the window into God's power in action as demonstrated in the lives of thousands of young students, many of whom have taken the flame of revival to the nations of the world.

Grams is more than a researcher; he is a witness to the amazing works of God. From the white-hot core of a revival spanning a quarter of a century, Grams' firsthand account demonstrates for us this revival's scope, its vibrancy, and its transforming power. *In Awe in Argentina* shows us God in action!

This book will surely make every reader hungrier for God!

—RICHARD NICHOLSON
DIRECTOR FOR LATIN AMERICA AND THE CARIBBEAN
ASSEMBLIES OF GOD WORLD MISSIONS

To the students of revival:
May God enhance your deep hunger for Him
and may He surprise you beyond imagination.

Acknowledgments

THIS BOOK HAS been a team project from the outset—fifteen years to think about it. I spent five years writing it, then God used Dr. Carolyn Tennant as a catalyst and motivator to make it come together. Her invaluable help in correcting and editing, helping the transitions to flow, and making things understandable will be a cherished memory.

My wife, Sherry, has helped clear my schedule many times and has given me counsel and inspiration throughout.

Our son, Nathan, projected the vision and got me writing five years ago.

Our daughter, Larisa, and son, Ben, have continually believed in this project of faith and expressed it often.

I am very grateful to my friend, Edgardo Muñoz, for his inspiration.

To my assistant, Carolina López Greco, for excellent proofreading and for the spiritual tone she afforded; to Cynthia Herrera and to Beatriz Zenone for their tenacity in contacting so many who gave testimony; to María Ester Alfieri for her faith and for the many hours of transcribing taped testimony.

How can I express my gratitude to the many pastors, evangelists and missionaries, protagonists of revival, who have given unselfishly of their time for interviews with the various revivals classes from North Central University and for personal conversations: Dante Gebel, Claudio Freidzon,

Carlos Annacondia, Pedro Ibarra, Edgardo Muñoz, Alberto Scataglini, José Manuel Carlos, Alberto Aranda, Hugo Weiss, Guillermo Prein, Osvaldo and Alejandra Carníval, Alberto Rey, Ralph Hiatt, Alberto Romay, Damián González, Rocco Di Trolio, and Eliana Nervegna.

I am also grateful to Dr. Grace Barnes of Azusa Pacific University for accepting this project as my capstone.

Contents

Foreword

ARGENTINA WAS A country I once knew very little about. I certainly did not know of its sophisticated European immigrant heritage, nor of its passionate love. As a professor and longtime student of revival history, I wondered what God was really doing in this country where revival seemed to be going on for decades. Stories are one thing, but experiencing them is another. So I took a group of students from my North Central University class to find out.

I soon realized I would never be the same. Strange, how a trip can change your life. The churches were alive, not asleep. They were growing and thriving, not struggling to find enough converts to baptize annually. There were testimonies—real ones, recent ones—of God's healing power, His miracles, and provision; of protection and the active operation of the gifts of the Holy Spirit.

Our missionary hosts were part of the impact. Rocky and Sherry Grams have been serving in Argentina for twenty-five years now, with Rocky now the Director (President) of Instituto Bíblico Rio de la Plata (IBRP). How was it they knew everybody? I soon realized that the majority had attended the school. The Gramses set up interviews for our group with people we would never have seen otherwise, and these were videotaped.

It was then that I knew Rocky had to write this book. He has the breadth of sight for the whole revival that few have. He knows so many people and has heard multitudes of the stories and testimonies. He is right there and has personally experienced what God is doing. His wisdom and insight about what was happening ran deep.

This book is the result of Rocky's meticulous journaling and recording over the years. He has interviewed so many people to get the firsthand accounts that are shared here. I am of the belief that you will be blessed by the combination of miraculous stories, thought-provoking commentaries, and interesting quotations from the revival's leaders throughout the pages of this book. These all intertwine to provide an exciting and easy read.

Sherry Grams is the instigator of their famous "pie nights" when she makes pies—all different kinds, mind you—for about twenty-five students who come to their home. They play games, but then they usually ask a revealing question. In the early eighties, at one of the first gatherings, they asked the group when was the last time they wept.

One of the students, Héctor Ferreyra, said, "On Thursday, for the lost in my city." Héctor would often dream of traveling to other countries to preach the gospel. He went on to pastor the church he founded with missionary Dick Nicholson and saw it quickly grow to three hundred members. Then he and his family, along with twenty-five workers, moved from the city of Rosario to the city of Neuquén to work alongside Steve and Jeri Hill in planting a church. Within a year that new church was running more than one thousand in attendance. That congregation in turn has mothered another fifty congregations. He is constantly traveling to many other countries and preaching with the anointing of the Spirit with signs following.

Such are the stories. The dreams and tears and prayers that started at IBRP have come to fruition and are changing the country of Argentina. This humble man, Rocky Grams, will undoubtedly affect you as he and his wife, Sherry, have in my various visits. The stories of the students, pastors, evangelists, and the lay people all weave an amazing tapestry and present a beautiful picture of God at work.

—CAROLYN TENNANT, PHD
PROFESSOR, NORTH CENTRAL UNIVERSITY
MINNEAPOLIS, MN
AUGUST 12, 2004

Preface

THIS BOOK WOULD not have been written had we not seen people running forward in an open field to accept Christ, students incapacitated to speak in their own language for days at a time, lines up to four blocks long to get into church, teeth miraculously filled by the power of God, limbs growing out, the demon-possessed freed by the hundreds, entire jails of Christian heart-washed prisoners, and up to one hundred thousand young people coming together at one time to declare their commitment to robust holiness in Christ. This book would not have been written had we not seen dozens of well-dressed and punctilious pastors falling in a heap on each other under the power of God, students sent flying up to fifteen feet by God's playfulness—had we not heard the groanings of the demon-possessed transformed into praises of Christ and laughter.

A revival is definitely a sovereign work of God—but He does not work in a vacuum. This is not a recipe book for revival, not a "how to cook up your own revival" manual. It is not a critique among connoisseurs of revival, nor do we want to pat ourselves on the back as fortunate residents of Argentina during these amazing years. This book is an attempt to obey God and write what we have seen and what we have lived. It is birthed after much thought and planning.

A portion of Psalm 105:2–5 has been singing in my heart for some time now, "Sing to him, sing praise to him; tell of all his wonderful acts ... let the hearts of those who seek the LORD rejoice ... Remember the wonders he has done." I will certainly be happy if reading these pages produces a greater measure of faith, spiritual hunger, and spontaneous praises of God. My prayer is that the Holy Spirit will take hold of your heart and lifestyle with the same tender, yet powerful, insistence that He has used with the human protagonists of this revival.

What did we do to deserve so much grace poured out? Nothing. Christ's love did it all. Yet He worked through willing vessels—especially those men and women who gave Him total control of their personal resources and agenda, not just for a roller-coaster season, but for years and for life. Without these key individuals, God's grace may not have been made known in such evident and memorable ways.

We usually can name many reasons why God cannot work in our town, city, church, culture, or family. Why has God's Spirit been allowed to work here in so many ways? Part of the answer is that the heart soil was prepared for the seed and there was the needed moisture for it to germinate.

May this book prepare your own heart and encourage you to have faith. Seeing what God has done, we can be assured He wants to work everywhere in all hearts, in all churches, and in all countries.

Introduction

J UST OVER A quarter century ago a freshman student walked
through the doors of Instituto Biblico Rio de la Plata for
her first day of class. She went to the chapel where the rest
of the newly arrived freshmen awaited, and in her determination to begin her first friendships she noticed one among
them all with a young looking face. "Are you a freshman here?"
she asked. "No, I've been here for a year already." The conversation was pleasant and lasted a couple of minutes until the
moment came to officially begin the school year.

The man with the young looking face was no less than
Rocky Grams, who had taken on the role of Director of the
Institute less than a year earlier. Many, including the student
who had been conversing moments before, were surprised
with the humility and little fanfare concerning his position,
the "alma mater" of the Institute.

Since then Rocky has not changed (not even his young
looking face), but there have been many inspiring experiences that have touched his heart. Along with his wife, Sherry,
they have helped the Bible Institute to become a place of eru-
dition and anointing at the same time. In the twenty-seven
years of their service here, IBRP has experienced a variety of
circumstances such as student overcrowding in times of spiritual harvest, periods of national economic crises, fads negat-
ing the usefulness of theological training institutes, and much
more. But its president has never lost the vision that God gave
him.

The fruit of his integrity, his seeking of God, his sensitivity and consistency have resulted in the training at IBRP of dozens of very well-known ministers and hundreds of outstanding pastors and leaders.

In our days we find many books that respond to the demand of emerging emphases. But this book is atypical because it crystallizes the author's feelings over years. To read *In Awe in Argentina* is to read the heart of Rocky Grams, but not only that, it means desiring a ministry of anointing, humility, and miracles.

I was about to leave on a long trip when the manuscript was placed in my hands. As I usually fall asleep very quickly on a flight I had little hope of finishing my reading of the book. But after the first glance I felt captivated and moved. I could not put it down until the last chapter.

Missionaries, professors, students of theological institutions, doctors of theology, pastors, and others have had similar experiences with the book. They only interrupted their reading to dry their tears and immerse themselves in prayer. I would not hesitate for an instant about recommending this book as a text for the subject of revivals for any seminary that seeks a very high level. Simply put, this is *In Awe in Argentina*.

—Edgardo Muñoz
Vice President, River Plate Bible Institute

1

The Twenty-Ninth Chapter of Acts

THE REVIVAL IN Argentina has lasted for decades with new waves flowing over this country. Many great pastors and evangelists have been a part of this move of God, but the story of the Argentine revival also includes the layperson and young people. So let's start there, with the testimonies of those who are just like you and me.

These testimonies are amazing. They pop up anywhere, just about every time a person turns around. It becomes a part of daily life here in Argentina. There is no Acts 29 in the Bible, but perhaps in a way, it is being written now by a God who is still doing great things through His church. Of course, these will never become part of holy Scripture, but God loves to keep telling His stories.

Each Monday morning in chapel at Instituto Bíblico Río de la Plata (IBRP), the River Plate Bible College students share what has just happened in their lives, usually that very weekend while they have been busily preaching and sharing the gospel. It is always exciting to watch their faces as they describe what God is doing.

Besides this, when we all go out for ministry and mingle with the pastors, we hear even more stories. Time is given for testimonies in the church services here. The people have so many examples of God's grace and provision. They get encouraged as their understanding of God's power and love increases. They ponder the stories and talk about the testimonies with their friends who are thereby introduced to a mighty, loving Father.

We are told that Satan will be overcome by the blood of the Lamb and by the word of our testimony. (See Revelation 12:11.) Testimony is uplifting and faith-building. It seems to generate trust.

Churches have had to limit the number of testimonies allowed in a service. Some pastors say, "Four and no more." But we end up having two or three beyond that from the nineteen who are running to the platform in hopes of being able to share.

Before the revival it might have been necessary to prepare a cliché like, "Who is the first brave person with a testimony?" During this move of God we have needed crowd control when testimonies are solicited. Now many of the pastors have their leaders listen to the testimonies in order to filter and sort them, then the individuals are chosen to give a synthesized version of the most outstanding.

All these different accounts pile into our lives, providing us with the big picture of an extremely active God. He is definitely on the move, changing lives, and touching people. There are so many stories that we recall, but here are a few vignettes from the world where God is clearly at work.

SOME TYPICAL MONDAY MORNING TESTIMONIES AT IBRP

A freshman, Luis, testified, "I came to the school with no money. They called me from the office and told me I had until today to bring in a minimum amount or I would have to leave. God told me to show up today. He said, 'The one who invites pays.' I was about to say goodbye to you all, but here is the Lord's provision." With that, he held up a wad of money. Then, with tears in his eyes, he stated various times, "Jehovah Jireh is here!"

↓

One young man said, "I asked God for one hundred souls this week. In our first open-air meeting seventy showed up. We held another and had over thirty. One hundred responded to accept Christ into their lives."

↓

"I put oil on my finger and put it into a young girl's ear," another student was saying. "Then I watched as Jesus healed her swollen neck and ruptured eardrum immediately!"

↓

"We looked all over for a geriatric home," said one young lady, "and finally found one with eighteen beautiful little grandmas in it. They think we're angels. 'Nobody ever hugs us,' they say, 'but you do.' Saturday, sixteen of the eighteen gave their hearts to Christ."

↓

One of our freshmen explained, "On our missions trip I preached five times. We went to a town forty-five kilometers into the mountains that could only be reached on mule-back or by walking. Starting at five o'clock, we walked fourteen hours with sixty-pound backpacks. It was so hot that it felt like we had heatstroke, but five people were saved in that town. Now we have to arrange for someone to go and pastor them."

↓

"Last night we showed the Jesus film, and twenty-seven people accepted Christ."

↓

"God told me to give a paralyzed man a swift kick. He was healed totally and instantly! I know that's unusual, but that's what happened."

↓

Another young man said, "I felt I should stop the van and tell the transvestite that Jesus loves him. I told him about the cross, and he opened his heart to Jesus. He had never known that kind of true love before."

↓

Walter testified of eleven who were healed at a campaign that he preached, including a ten-year-old deaf, mute girl.

↓

Karina said the vacation time between classes had been hard, and she almost had not returned to school. But there she was, and she had decided to join the Children's Evangelism Team. That weekend they had gone out in ministry. There was a sixteen-year-old girl at the railroad, ready to take her own life, when the clowns from the team showed up near the station. "I'll go watch the clowns as a last act," the girl had thought. But that day the clowns shared the gospel message, and the young woman accepted Christ. That weekend her mother and brother and sister all became Christians along with eighty other adults and children in that town.

PRAYING FOR THE MOST DESPERATE

Pastor Alberto shared these two testimonies of God's amazing and timely work:

On Friday, a distraught man and his wife walked into church. The man had been kicked out of his house a few days before by his stepson who had recently returned from law school. In the chaos and violence of that moment, he confessed to his wife the reason for her son's disdain and anger toward him. Twenty years before, when they had been married just three years, he had raped her son. Now the hideous act had come back to haunt him.

In his desperation, the man had taken a dagger and stabbed himself twice just below the heart. When he was released from the hospital, he and his wife had been walking down the street, very upset. The man kept repeating, "There is no way out for me." Then they heard in their minds a voice telling them the name of Pastor Alberto's church. They had never heard of it, but looked it up and came that Friday night.

The pastor talked with them and led them to the Lord, and they asked each other's forgiveness. The woman had lived a joyless marriage for twenty years following their first three years together. She never had understood the abrupt change. Finally she knew why.

Now he was afraid to go back to the house, but she insisted. When his violent stepson, who had expelled him and sworn he would never leave the house, saw them at the door arm in arm, he grabbed his things and moved out of the house. A marriage was saved.

The clincher of this testimony is that Pastor Alberto's church had been praying specifically for the most desperate and hopeless people of their community, people who feel there is no way out. God brought them another such difficult case that very same week.

Pastor Alberto always tries to take Monday off, but that Monday he felt they needed to go to the church. His wife asked why, but he had no answer. When they arrived there, a man was waiting, standing stooped over his motorcycle. He asked to come into the church and pray. Cautious because of the five robberies they have sustained at the church, they nonetheless started talking to the man who said that he had just come from an overpass where he had tried to take his life. But something had stopped him, and he had heard a voice in his mind saying the name of their church. He had never heard of it before, but here he was at the door, wanting to pray.

What were the reasons for his desperation? After an argument with his wife, out of spite, he had attempted to rape one of their daughters. Thankfully, his wife had walked in on them. He felt that neither his wife nor his two daughters could ever forgive him. In remorse and self-loathing, he had decided to take his own life. He had moved out and lost hope of ever being back with his family. The man had been totally convinced that there was no way out for him. God worked a miracle. After praying with Pastor Alberto, he accepted Christ. His wife called that day and put his daughters on the phone. They told him they wanted to see him. God is transforming him. Pastor Alberto has already seen him three times this week!

Healing is on the way for both of these men and their families. Forgiveness is possible in Christ.

A Little Missions Trip to a Rough Neighborhood

It got very quiet in the car. When we turned right we had run out of pavement and suddenly we were driving in deep mud, a street full of potholes with groups of sinister-looking guys standing around on both sides looking in at us with interest and some surprise. It was our first time out in this quarter with the ministerial team, and we were in two vehicles with mostly freshmen on this team, including some attractive young ladies. No wonder it had gotten quiet in the car.

When we got our bearings, doubled back and turned left, there it was—a large shed-type building half a block away from that wrong turn. About three hundred people were singing up a storm inside, and it seemed like an island of peace in the midst of a very dangerous neighborhood.

The service went well. At midnight people were still asking us to pray for their tremendous needs and heartache. What a great opportunity for the students. Pastors Abraham and Monica had prepared pizza and sausage sandwiches (*choripanes*) for us after the service and started to share testimonies.

Monica was the one with the strong burden to start a church. She began praying for women at her Mary Kay meetings. When more than sixty women showed up, her husband suspected something. She had planted a church, using the sale of cosmetics as a cover.

Abraham's parents had been evangelists and his family had suffered so much lack that he had sworn he would never be in ministry. But how do you close down a church after it has been birthed? They also began a Christian bookstore, and they came to expect the many people who streamed in to inquire and then were delivered from demons.

↓

Pastor Abraham shared that they have two hundred recovered drug addicts in their church.

Twenty of them have jobs with the city in an anti-drug program where they can make a difference and talk about Jesus. There is a team in the church that has put together a bakery, and various families have income from it. These are viable alternatives to delinquency. The church has a radio program and cable TV program, and it is impacting that whole area.

One day a drug lord who felt convicted by their testimonies went to the church specifically to kill the pastor. As the man was getting out of his car, he heard a voice say: "*A este no lo mates* (Don't kill this one)". The man got back in his car and left. Now he is part of the church.

↓

During one service, the offering was being received and a young delinquent had come off the street to rob. As he put his hand in his pocket the pastor thought, "How nice. This new guy is going to give a coin in the offering."

Just then, Pastor Monica reached out and touched the young man on the head. The man went sprawling, and the gun he was about to draw careened across the floor. The people from the congregation quickly recovered the weapon and prayed for him so the service would not be interrupted.

↓

One young man would give up to eight hundred dollars at a time of tithes in the offering. When the deacon asked him about it, he would say, "I work" or "Things are going well." In one Sunday service, he had no money at offering time, so he told the deacon he would be right back. Within twenty minutes he returned with a large offering.

"Where did you get that money?" the leader asked him.

"I went out and did a job," was the answer.

"What kind of job?"

"A stick-up."

"What do you mean?"

"Yes, God protects me." He was in partnership with an individual with many contacts and had been sharing the loot fifty-fifty.

Astounded, the church leader said he would pray for a situation where this would end. One Sunday the man had received a tip that there was an almost-new light blue truck to steal at a certain address. He and his partner accosted the driver at gunpoint. The victim was a well-dressed guy in a tie who asked if he could get his documents out of the glove compartment. "Sure," the young man answered. When the man did retrieve his documents, he also grabbed a Bible.

"So you're a Christian?"

"Yes, I'm a pastor."

"Wow, where?"

"Of this church." The pastor motioned behind them, and there was much of the congregation staring in consternation out of the windows at the scene of their pastor being held up.

The young man forgot himself and said cheerfully, "I'm a Christian, too." Looking at the congregation with a big grin, he waved at them, forgetting that he was holding a revolver in that hand!

"Listen, Pastor, my partner is nervous. I have to take this truck, but I'll park it right around the corner and leave everything intact and the keys on the seat, OK?" That day he went back to church and truly surrendered his life to Christ. Today, he is a policeman who goes out once a week to find drug addicts in the most desperate situations to take to the Monday evening special meetings they have to rescue extreme cases. The week we were there they had brought in a drug addict who was injecting into a raw patch of flesh on his leg—straight into the tendons.

Our students learned a great deal about ministry that night, and what a church! It truly is an oasis in the midst of chaos and violence—a hospital for broken people. What a gospel of Christ's power and practical love.

The Making of a Pastor

A disorderly lifestyle and much alcohol consumption brought Bartolomé to the place where the doctors diagnosed him with cirrhosis of the liver and gave him just six months to live. He told his wife, who had prayed for his salvation faithfully for twelve years, that he was going out in style; that his plan was to die with a glass of wine or whiskey in his hand.

As a building contractor with dozens of people working for him, he was doing very well financially and had no intention of asking for help or seeking God. He sold off his ten trucks, his machinery, tractors, and bulldozer and gave half of the money to his wife. The other half was quickly being wasted away. But one night, though he was dead drunk, something told him that he had to go to the Carlos Annacondia campaign. His son and daughter found him there. As he listened to the evangelist preach, he would insult him until his twelve-year-old son ended up crying.

Suddenly he saw over a thousand people running toward the altar. Annacondia would pray and people would cry out and fall on the ground, but drunken Bartolomé was still standing. The evangelist took a break and then said, "If you have an incurable disease, God wants to heal you today." His daughter begged him to raise his hands. "God won't charge you anything," she said. She and her brother were both crying until he finally raised his hands just to please them. When he did, he felt a powerful whirlwind. It was sent by God and knocked him flat on his face in the muddy ditch. As he wiped the mud off his eyes, he realized he was healed. Bartolomé, a man who never cried, began to weep with joy.

Three days later he was already helping to cast out demons in the Annacondia "intensive care" tent. He would just listen to what a believer with authority was saying and do the same. Now he is a pastor. It has been eighteen years since the healing, and he still has perfect health.

The church Pastor Bartolomé is pastoring today is known as a powerful hospital for souls. One day a police car drove up and two policemen dragged a writhing man into the church. They had him tied and chained, both feet and hands. One of the policemen, a Christian, said, "The judge told us to take him to Romero (the insane asylum). But I know that his problem is not insanity. He is bound by demons so we brought him here."

"Let him go," said the pastor. At first the policemen would not. Finally, when he insisted, with trembling hands they untied and unshackled him. "In the name of Jesus, be loosed," the pastor commanded, and suddenly the man opened his eyes and asked, "Where am I? Why am I in a church?" This man is serving Christ today.

The Lives of Bible College Students

People who visit, tend to look at the faces of our students in worship, hear their prayers, and see their commitment, and then come to a conclusion about these "saints." Some of the real stories, though, are surprising evidence of God's grace.

Miguel, a police officer, had been living with three women simultaneously other than his wife. He was smoking three to four packs of cigarettes a day. Once as he was dropping his wife off at an evangelistic meeting, he turned to leave and was knocked to the floor by the power of God. Immediately the cigarette habit was broken, and his home was restored. He came to IBRP and by the time he was a sophomore, he was already preaching on secular radio. God has used him to heal a quadriplegic of twenty years. He prayed over the telephone with one lady, and her varicose veins were healed. Would-be suicide victims have come to Christ. Well-known singers and artists are accepting the Lord under his ministry. It has been quite a turn-around!

↓

Carina was a drug addict raised in a leprosarium because her mother is affected by the disease. As a teenager she went to live with her aunt who was very involved in spiritism. One day she looked at the various witchcraft images in the corner of her room and said, "God, consume it all." The next day everything was burned up. The images of plaster were destroyed, and the wood nearby was scorched. Only her notebooks remained untouched. As a student at IBRP, she asked God to send her to preach in the jails or places where others do not want to go. Today she is married to the pastor of a church of more than one thousand two hundred people in our largest jail.

↓

There are so many other student testimonies. Adrián was a highway robber who stole trucks, sold and consumed drugs, and lived in the fast lane until Christ transformed his life.

↓

Myriam Psocik, a pretty, blue-eyed young lady of Ukrainian descent, had been diagnosed with terminal cancer. One day she spit up to a quart of blood and infectious fluid. She was so weak she could not even hold a broom. But there she was at IBRP, totally healed by the power of Jesus.

↓

Alejandro Hernández was in a cult for ten years, but then his girlfriend witnessed to him. His mother was also healed. A nurse, she had been medicating her own stomach disorders for years, and the closets of the house overflowed with pills. In one week the Lord healed his mother completely, and in the next year she won one hundred fifty people to Christ through her personal testimony. Alejandro had a tremendous burden to evangelize to his own country of Uruguay and now is planting a church there.

↓

Juan, a pastor's son, was about to throw himself under a train. Remembering that his father had asked for a Bible school application for him, he postponed his fateful decision and filled out the application. He had been totally resistant to the idea and had scoffed at his older brother for attending that place "of sissies, where people cry." Little did we know why he was so broken and wept for hours on end that first week of classes. Now he preaches with tenderness and authority, and people decide for Christ every time.

↓

Mariano Rosato said that he was very troubled before he met the Lord. He went to the cemetery every morning at three or four o'clock to "talk with his mother." One day, he watched his girlfriend slit her wrists. Both of them were high on drugs when someone handed them a leaflet, an invitation to an evangelistic campaign. He somehow found his way to that meeting. As a former rock magazine reporter with hair to his waist and weighing less than one hundred pounds, he was little more than a skeleton. But the power of God became real for him that day, and when he gave his life to Christ, he saw the drug addiction, the mental anguish, the sickness, and the weakness all fall away. God is using him and his wife, another graduate of IBRP.

WHERE SHOULD THE CHURCH MEET?

It has been exciting to watch the God-inspired originality of so many pastors and leaders concerning meeting places for their churches. Congregations have had their services in the open air, homes, beat-up tents, an abandoned railroad car, hotels, factories, clubs, dance halls, and restaurants. New church plants are being started all the time, so it is necessary to get creative.

I have preached in the dead of winter with almost freezing temperatures in places that had no windows or heat— the church was under construction. We could see our breath as we worshiped God!

↓

This past week I was teaching and preaching at a men's retreat for the Hurlingham Church where Héctor Manzolido is the pastor. Six years ago they were renting a hall and had outgrown it. One day the youth of the church walked across the plaza to an empty theater that was all boarded up. They placed their hands on those boards and prayed, claiming the place by faith for the church. Less than a year later, the owner loaned them the theater for one night. That got extended, and the church has used it free of charge—except for property taxes—for five years now. Seven or eight people accept Christ every Sunday. The owner does not totally understand why he is being so generous toward them, but his architectural business has been immensely blessed by God during these five years.

↓

The Rey de Reyes Church meets in a former ice skating rink. They have purchased most of the square block at enormous expense and sacrifice and have now built a new sanctuary, since the crowds extend around the block to be able to get into the building for a service. Their previous steps of faith to pick up one house at a time on that block is now allowing them to move forward into their new space. Additionally, God had perfect timing for them. The owner of one of the biggest pieces of land they needed kept delaying in closing the deal. When the Argentine economy crashed later, he was willing to sell for half. Also the church's money was being held in U.S. dollars, allowing the savings to go even farther. God has His ways of providing.

↓

After months of setting up one hundred fifty wooden chairs at a wide place on the sidewalk by the subway entrance, the Federal Capital Church walked to a car garage and offices that the Lord had provided. The church has since purchased the textile factory next door and an industrial dry cleaning center, and with this newly remodeled space is now running over fifteen thousand people.

↓

Avance Cristiano started a church in a garage and later rented a pornographic movie theater for a while. They had to cover up the movie advertising with brown paper every time they met. Now they are in a former warehouse and have purchased land nearby that contains a halfbuilt, abandoned industrial building.

↓

A new church plant by our dean of students, Ernesto Nanni, is now located in an old carpenter's shop. The walls and floor were covered in a greasy type of film, and missions teams from the States helped to scrub it all off and give it a fresh coat of paint. Recently there was a prophetic word that where the grease had been there would now flow the oil of the Spirit, and it would turn into a river moving out into the community.

↓

The Mar del Plata Church is in a very large old downtown movie theater. Other churches meet in little storefronts or anywhere they can find. The churches rise up so fast that it is always a challenge to locate a place for them.

↓

A new church being planted right now by IBRP students in the Capital Plaza does not even have a building yet. They meet outside in the park across from the train station, dealing with being robbed and mugged. But the gospel is going forth in the center of this city of thirteen million, and the church is growing. Their first two-day campaign resulted in forty-five decisions for Christ. The church just keeps moving out—two prostitutes one day, five cross-dressers the next, five more prostitutes, and many others who have committed their lives to the One who loves winos and sinners. Their multiple cell groups are moving into neighbors' garages and homes.

They have the largest church building in the world. They have no walls, and the sky is their roof. The pulpit is standing up on a round cement park table. I wonder where they will end up.

A New Church Full of Former Drug Addicts

I recently visited the church of one of our graduates, Juan Ramón. This young man had come out of the drug culture, and I remember well his sold-out attitude as a student. Once a quarter we hold a picnic in a public park with the whole student body. Instead of playing soccer—a national pastime here—or drinking *mate* (green herbal tea) with his friends, Juan would sit with the spectators in the park who had come to watch our games, and share his faith with them.

My visit was on the one-year anniversary of the church that he planted and the church was made up of a corrugated tin roof and walls, gaping spaces covered over with curtains, and a one-toilet bathroom with no running water. Their building is not in very good shape, but their congregation certainly is.

The celebration lasted from eleven o'clock to almost midnight. When I arrived, a young man was giving his testimony. He said, "I never received one 'I love you' or a hug from my dad. They beat me and kicked me out of the house. Now my life is totally different."

↓

A second young man began to share. "I was despised by my parents before my birth," he said. He went on to explain that he had been beaten with sticks, and his father would hit his mother also. Then one day the police killed his dad. Seething with frustration and anger, he began to participate in armed robberies.

"It was like there was a voice within me that controlled me," he said. "I destroyed many people, and often I had shoot-outs with the police."

One day the young man got angry with his older brother and did not speak to him for five years. Even his uncle mistreated him and would chase him with a knife.

After he got married, he would hit his wife also. When she asked him if he loved her, he would answer, "What does it mean to love?"

"The pastor prayed for me," he said in his testimony, "and something unattached itself from me. It was the demons. I gave my life to God, and He helped me forgive the man who killed my father. Now I can say to my mother, 'I love you.' God kept me from the bullets. He kept me from the overdoses. God loves me." God was teaching him to love his whole family, including his wife. At that moment I watched as the pastor walked up and hugged him. They wept for a long time together.

Pastor Juan Ramón started with two people a year ago and now has more than two hundred in the church. Drug addicts spend the night, pouring out their frustrations to him, and he leads them to Christ. Talk about love. Talk about fruit!

Some Unusual Approaches to Evangelism

At a men's retreat one weekend I talked to a man who was cooking up a fresh approach to evangelism. He is a master chef and shared with me the idea God gave him. Frustrated at the number of times his friends and neighbors had rejected his invitations to attend services, he asked the pastor if he could offer free baking classes at the church. Nineteen have signed up. Before he starts each class he talks about the sweetness of Jesus and then shows them how to bake pastries and cakes and other such delicacies. So far, seven of the students have accepted the Lord. One of them has brought in two backsliders. Not bad for a cooking class.

↓

Pastor Alberto Aranda shared about two ladies from his congregation who walked up to a man on the street and exclaimed, "You need God!" He pulled out a knife and told them he was on his way to commit suicide because he had AIDS. They took the knife and accompanied the man to church. He is attending faithfully.

↓

As the economic situation has worsened here in Argentina, the crisis is bringing an increase in stealing, armed robberies, and kidnappings. Stories abound. Even pets are being kidnapped and held for ransom.

One Christian couple continued to live in a ghetto-like area despite God's abundant blessing on their lives. They had neighbors who had trained up their children to steal, and had even given two of their sons exactly the same name to confuse the judicial process. This family broke into their house to steal so many times that the Christian couple finally decided to leave and move to an apartment. However, they also kept their old house in that rough neighborhood and transformed it into a feeding-program base. Today some of those very children of the neighbors are being fed and kept alive by their former robbery victims. That certainly is turning the other cheek!

↓

A teenager trying to steal a bicycle was shot so many times in the legs by the father of the child riding it that he had both legs amputated. Christians visited him in the hospital to show him love, despite his guilty-as-charged situation, and he responded to their love.

God's Protection

One of our church members, Néstor Pavia, testified that he had left church after a Saturday evening service and got off the bus in a very dark area near a religious image. He felt like singing a praise chorus, so he did. There were two men standing in the shadows, one on each side of the image. As he continued to walk past, he heard one say, "Grab him. What are you waiting for?"

His partner in crime answered, "No! Can't you tell that he is an evangelical?"

As we were rejoicing over this testimony, Pastor Edgardo Muñoz mentioned another situation that also happened with Néstor a while back. He was riding home from work one evening with meal tickets in his backpack. During this time of economic crisis, many companies do not pay their workers actual money; they pay them vouchers or tickets instead.

As he was about to ride across a bridge, he noticed a pregnant woman. Suddenly a man stepped out from behind her and jammed a gun into the back of his neck, trying to pull the backpack off at the same time. Suddenly Néstor felt a strong push from behind, and he sailed on past the man. The next thing Néstor heard was the trigger being pulled, but the gun did not fire.

He continued on his way—happy for the protection of God.

↓

A lady from Pastor Alberto Aranda's church was being held up at gunpoint by a thief working alone one day. "What's the matter?" she asked him. "Do you have a family and you can't get a job? Is that why you're out holding people up?" As the thief assented, she stated with authority, "Put that gun away. Let's talk." As the surprised robber stared at her and obediently put the gun down, she offered, "You can't get a job? Come to my church and bring your family. We'll get you a job." The young man did just that, and he and his entire family accepted Christ.

↓

Our worship leader, Diego Avalos, was being held up once. "I spoke to them about Jesus," he stated, "and one of the robbers began to say in a trembling voice, 'Jesus...Jesus...Jesus.' Suddenly, the robber started shaking and the gun fell to the ground."

↓

Another member of our church was being held up, and as he looked down the barrel of the gun, he commanded, "In the name of Jesus, stop." The thief obeyed!

↓

Pablo, an IBRP student, was walking to church when he suddenly felt a strong impression to lift his hands and praise God in song. So he did. It was at that moment that some thieves had come up behind him to steal his leather jacket at gunpoint. "What are you singing about?" they asked. He shared his testimony with them, starting with the fact that a while back he had also "worked the streets."

"Sorry, man," they apologized. "We didn't realize it." He shared Christ with them and invited them to the school to visit him.

↓

A teenager looking for a good time tried to proposition one of the young ladies from the Mar del Plata church as she waited for a bus late at night after the service had finished. When she told him she was an evangelical Christian, he drove off, exclaiming in exasperation, "I can't believe it. You are the third *evangélica* I have come across tonight!"

Consternation in the Constitution Train Station

One Saturday in my freshman evangelism class, a student told about a number of them going down to a main train station to share their faith in Christ. Due to the very desperate situation the nation is facing economically, there are many homeless people living in the station. As these young people opened their hearts concerning God's love, one of them noticed an unkempt man standing there in an extremely dirty shirt, tattered and worn and full of the stench of urine. The student had recently been given a new silk shirt and was wearing it that day. *Give him your shirt,* he sensed God say. Immediately, he took off his new shirt and handed it to the wanderer. Looking at it in his hands, the man began to weep, removed his own shirt, and handed it to the young man who had been standing there bare-chested. Our student put on the stench-filled shirt and hugged the man. Passers-by were so moved, they wept at such a demonstration of love. They knelt right there and with tears accepted Christ as Savior.

An Evangelistic Bridge

Not too long ago I handed Gastón, a sophomore student at River Plate Bible Institute, one hundred dollars of Light-for-the-Lost funds as seed for his wild dream of selling Bibles. He wanted to use this as an opportunity to reach those who do not know Christ. That amount in Bibles will be donated to needy individuals during the course of this program. In less than a month, Gastón and another young Christian have already seen much fruit. More than two hundred have accepted Christ. What evident hunger for the Word during a time of economic stress in Argentina. God is at work.

↓

The IBRP students learned that among the two hundred newly born-again inmates of the maximum security prison in Olavarría, only sixty had Bibles. Strapped for funds themselves, the students sacrificially supplied almost all the Bibles that were needed.

God Is Giving Us Laughter at This Time

Another student shared that she had always been wary of people's accounts of the demonstrations of God's power. "But," she stated, "I laughed so hard at church until three thirty this weekend. I have never laughed so heartily in all my life—for an entire hour." When she mentioned it with some embarrassment to one of the church leaders, he answered that he had no problem believing it because the pastor's daughter had laughed for three hours that same week.

When so many people are full of venom and anger, laughter stands out as a sign from God.

Off to Paraguay

A while ago, I accompanied seventeen graduates to Pilar Neembucú, Paraguay, a town of about forty thousand that was a twenty-hour bus ride north. On the little ferry to the other side of the river between Argentina and Paraguay, the students had already led two people to Jesus.

By the time ten days were up, they had shared their testimonies on three radio stations and in various schools, preaching simultaneous campaigns that included two nights in the plaza. There were healings, baptisms in the Holy Spirit, conversions, commitments to the call, and even deliverance from satanic power. One of the students grew up in that town and opened up the way for the team to share one bathroom and sleep on the church floor.

NOW TO HONDURAS

Most of the twenty-five students who had recently gradu-ated went on a missions trip to Honduras and had never even flown in an airplane. It took a lot of faith and eigh-teen months for them to raise the money to go. With all the prayer and work beforehand, their expectations were high. They started singing choruses in the airport between flights, and five people accepted Christ.

The students went on the radio for an hour during their first day in Honduras. Then they prayed with the mayor of the city of Cortés. Next came a television opportunity for an hour. Students boarded thirty-six public buses and shared their testimonies with people coming to Christ. One stu-dent gave his shoes and socks to a street urchin, and others prayed with people in the hospital. Some counseled rape vic-tims, with tears of healing flowing as people said they had never before told anyone. Graduates preached to hurricane victims, and one hundred ten people accepted the Lord that afternoon. Rice and beans were served for breakfast and iguana soup for lunch—it was God at work.

EVANGELISM CLASS

Recently I invited an evangelist to share testimonies of God's power in my evangelism class. He started ministering in the class. A young lady was healed of two cysts. Leonard Campbell from Honduras had two cavities filled and two teeth recon-stituted. When he told his mother on the phone, she accused him of wanting to avoid the dentist, but he assured her that they were completely taken care of by the best dentist of all. Those two fifty-minute classes lasted from four thirty to well past nine.

The evangelism students get hands-on practice, and the results are tremendous. Martin shared a while ago how he had spoken with his sister and his mother, and they accepted Christ the same day.

The Bible college students have a favorite pastime. It is not playing video games or watching movies. Instead, it is evangelism. They go out any time, all the time really, to share their faith. Perhaps this is why there are so many testimonies. They get out there, where the people are. Five saved here and two there; eighty or a hundred in a campaign. They help churches flood their neighborhoods with the Word, prayer, and witness. And just as the Book of Acts showed us the church being built up and established, so it is evident that the mighty God of the universe is continuing to advance His kingdom today. He uses all kinds of people, even unlikely ones; people just like you and me.

Wrap-Up

There is no doubt that God is still doing great things today. He uses all types of people to show forth His glory. It is not just the big names that God is moving through. It is the freshman Bible college student and the layperson in the church as well as the pastor and the evangelist. In the midst of every day practical living, God is showing Himself strong. In Argentina everybody who is serving God seems to have fresh testimonies on an on-going basis. God Himself is at work!

How did these sorts of things come about? What has been happening in Argentina to bring such testimonies of God's grace? It has been a long history, and an exciting one.

2

Waves of Revival

As we look back over twenty years of continuous revival here in Argentina and many more moves of the Lord before that, we are in awe of what God has done. He has chosen to pour out His power so extravagantly on our adoptive land. Why did He select Argentina to shake and bless so greatly? Why has this country been favored with so many waves of revival? It really has not stopped for decades.

How is it that a nation famous for its arrogance could be chosen by God to participate in one of the longest-lasting revivals in the history of the church? This is a culture of extreme sensuality: among the highest proportionately in the world for sales of negligeés, undergarments, and perfumes. The nation arguably has the shortest mini-skirts on the planet, and imposing sexual advertising is everywhere. The cult to body aesthetics has resulted in extremely high percentages of anorexia and bulimia. How could all this be the milieu for the powerful move of God's Spirit that has made us extremely sensitive to even the smallest sins of thought or motive?

"God is sovereign, and He decided to bless an unlikely nation" is only half the answer. The truth of the matter is that His power is available to any nation that seeks Him. Often His move that has sought to pour out revival has been ignored or misunderstood. So perhaps it would be useful to consider the context and characteristics of this nation to see what we can learn before we take a look at the history of the revival itself.

Openness to Spiritual Things

A large volume could be written on superstition in Argentina, along with witchcraft, nominal Christianity, the cult to pleasure, and the physical body. Circumstances in the nation's development have resulted in a country that is open to all kinds of spiritual perspectives.

Argentina is a very European country, with 97 percent of the population coming from that background. Of those, the majority are of Italian or Spanish extraction, and the rest are mostly German, British, Ukranian, and Slavic. The buildings and plazas in downtown Buenos Aires are beautiful, reminding one of European world-class cities. For decades, the nation was considered the United States of Latin America, achieving wealth and economic growth that seemed to open up unlimited potential. At the beginning of the twentieth century, the country was among the richest in the world in gold reserves and had the largest middle class of Latin America. The children of the elite studied in Europe, and threw so much money around that a popular saying of that time was "Rich as an Argentine."

But the apparent world-class power and prestige was lost, and the country is now filled with stories of dreams that came to nothing—of "paradise lost." The economic crash has affected everyone. Many have taken refuge in the help of psychiatrists or para-psychologists. The country has the highest ratio in the world of psychologists/mental health counselors to population. There are one hundred professionals for every 100,000 where there are only 25 to 45 in developed countries.[1] For the city of Buenos Aires, the ratio is one-in-200. People have entered deep depressions, some lasting for years. The result of hope is not just deferred but abandoned. Defrauded with the promises of corrupt leaders, some have tried to find solace in the sanctuaries of various Catholic virgins, others in voodoo-type religions or spiritism. The America's Confederation of Spiritism was founded in Buenos Aires.[2] New Age, yoga, and other modern escapist techniques are also in evidence. It is a nation in flux, seeking answers beyond the unbearable here and now.

Umbanda is the name of a religion based in Brazil with roots in Africa. The rites involved with this religion include sacrificing chickens and spreading bottles of oil in front of the house of a person's enemy. The focus of many of these ceremonies is to cast a spell on another person who is hated for having wronged them. Even well-to-do people are involved in this cult, some of them undertaking monthly trips of two thousand miles or more to see their *pae*, or spiritual father, in Brazil. Many of the *paes* coordinate male prostitution rings and attempt to use their spiritual powers to affect the will of many unsuspecting travelers of the night. We have had the children and grandchildren of *paes* as students at the Bible school. Some of them were ostracized from their families and curses cast on them when they gave their lives to Jesus.

Amazing as it may seem in a nation that at one time had as many as six versions of the daily newspaper, numerous high class universities, nuclear physicists and economists, educators of world-renown, and the largest yearly book fair of Latin America, superstition is still alive and well. In fact, Argentina has the third highest number of universities, exceeded only by India and the United States. In spite of all that is available to them, Argentines are seeking reality beyond their day-to-day life and often look to fetishes, such as San Cayetano, who is supposed to bring good luck for finding work. *La Difunta Correa* has shrines on many of the highways of the interior, despite the efforts of the Catholic church to stamp out the veneration of this woman, found dead still suckling her child. Gilda, a young singer who died at a young age, also has many shrines and followers, as does Rodrigo, *El Potro* (The Stallion), another singer who died in an automobile accident and who is still idolized today.

While traveling many of the roads, especially in the provinces of Misiones and Entre Ríos, one can observe many shrines filled with red ribbons. They are in veneration of *El Gauchito Gil.* This superstitious movement honors a defender of the poor at the sake of the rich, along the lines of Robin Hood. Many make yearly pilgrimages to the city of San Nicolás or to Luján to pay homage to the patron saints of these communities.

In a recent testimony, a reporter and popular sportscaster spoke of his life before accepting Christ and asked, "Who hasn't gone to a little witch?" In fact, a recent book entitled *Argentina Embrujada* (Bewitched Argentina) documents the use of witchcraft among the highest government officials of the nation up until 1995.[3]

BOLDNESS

One of the characteristics of the Argentine people is boldness, considered by some to be close to brashness. This personal trait is partly due to the effects of big city life. One third of the nation lives in Buenos Aires, a city of thirteen million, and there are other cities of around one million or more inhabitants. Ninety percent of the nation is urbanized. Also, by and large, the population is new to the land, being sons and daughters or grandchildren of immigrants. The *qué será, será* attitude of fatalism is not one espoused by those who have been willing to leave all they know in order to carve out a new life in an unknown land.

When inflation hit 100 percent or even 1000 percent annually, peoples' attitudes were not to crawl into a cave and let themselves die, it was to go out and find a way to survive. Many households had three or four breadwinners cooperating to make ends meet. Some couples took up to five full- and part-time jobs between them.

This "We'll find a way" attitude has affected the church

also: "We'll find a way to receive from God what they are receiving across town. Lord, I want that power, too!"

A bold move was evidenced during the early days of the first Carlos Annacondia campaigns when hundreds of pastors cancelled all services at their own church facilities and moved the congregation to participate nightly in the evangelistic campaigns for up to fifty days in a row.

ADAPTABILITY

Another part of this Argentine context is the adaptability of the people. Argentines have learned to make do with the difficult surprises of life for a few years now. Third in the world in gold reserves after World War II, Argentina had a per capita rate that was among the highest in the world in 1900. At the end of World War I, Argentina was the eleventh largest trading nation worldwide. Today the nation has been affected by a series of crises and years of monthly double-digit inflation. These have sapped the strength of the nation and changed high expectations into deep despondency. Sometimes inflation has been 140 percent in just one month! At a particular moment of economic crisis in 1989, there were announcements made in certain grocery stores that "Everything in your carts is now worth 40 percent more." People would tip their carts over and walk out in frustration. When we wanted to remember what the price of bread had been a year before, we would just take a zero off the present price. There were couples who would take out a loan to do simple maintenance, like putting windows and doors in their house, and due to inflation they would end up having to sell the house to pay their debts. The people have learned to adjust to adverse situations; to adapt.

During those years of hyperinflation, many times it was the believing family that was able to make ends meet—and a strong testimony was evident to all their acquaintances. On the other hand, there were moments that out of seven or eight in a family, only two could go to church because they could not afford the bus money for more to attend. They made adjustments.

For many years it was extremely difficult for lower- or middle-class families to even dream of having a new car. Vehicles had to be prepaid with up to forty-eight monthly payments before they could be driven off the lot. With ninety-six people paying in a cooperative agreement, two cars could be delivered each month, one by lot and the other to the highest bidder among those in the "payment circle." Even a payment plan like this demonstrates the creative adaptability evident in this culture. For a while we were all high financiers—either one understood the economy or he lost everything.

This characteristic of adaptability has been crucial in the nation's openness to the move of God. Argentine pastors have been very open to learn. They have adapted methods, structures, and ministerial emphases to what will work in their own communities.

Here in Argentina the dance clubs open for teens at eleven o'clock—and long lines form hours ahead of this—with the partying going into the early hours of the morning. I have seen churches that begin their youth ministry time at midnight on Friday evenings. The young people spend those nights at the church during the same hours that they used to be at the dance halls. Now the time is spent together in prayer, praise, table games, and sports activities. When the tragic nightclub fire occurred in Buenos Aires recently where scores of young people died and were injured, within just minutes one of the churches had four hundred church members there to help minister. Argentines step into the openings they are given.

Other congregations have hundreds of people break out into cell groups at one o'clock on Fridays, where they spend time together in sharing, training, and prayer. The willingness to adjust has been such an important part of this move of God.

Such openness to change has also been demonstrated in the Argentine acceptance of new musical forms. The traditional, folkloric, and *cumbia* were the normal music styles of the campaign years. Now there is a strong move to have a variety of musical styles, especially melodic rock and some blues. In comparison to countries like France and Italy, Argentina readily accepts foreign words as a part of its lexicon. This has meant that the music is being constantly renovated, and this has had an immense effect on the move of God, keeping it fresh and in touch with anointed artists.

Deference

Driving in this country is a wild experience. There is no such thing as a lane in actuality, and people do many unusual things, while driving aggressively. They don't even use horns; it is illegal except in a great emergency. But the drivers make it because of an interesting Argentine trait: deference.

That same deference, which allows the creative flow of traffic on the streets and avenues of Buenos Aires, is what has allowed the creative flow of the Holy Spirit's power. The revival has not been relegated to one little geographic pocket, nor was it placed in a time bubble that burst as soon as the euphoria wore off. Rather the people have given way to the Spirit over and over, all around the nation.

It has been deference again that allows each key personality of the revival to be without personal pretense and that has drawn mega-church pastors to pray together and attend each other's special meetings.

Just as we have learned to let God be God, we have discovered how to let Carlos Annacondia minister in his gifting the way God gave it to him and with the distinctive coloring of his own personality. We don't expect Sergio Scataglini to act like Claudio Freidzon or vice-versa, and we accept them all as they are.

The Concept of Waves

In an interview the North Central University revivals class had with Pastor Edgardo Muñoz, President of Assemblies of God Christian Education for Argentina and Vice President of IBRP, he presented several novel and practical concepts regarding the move of God here in Argentina.

Pastor Edgardo likes to look at our revival history as coming in waves, with each wave leaving its residue of blessing. He says, "These waves move off and leave a great deal of important sedimentation. After each revival the church is not the same."

This image is excellent for understanding revival history here in Argentina. There have been times in which God moved in amazing ways. This sent out ripple effects, splashed out—sometimes receded a bit, but then came in again as a fresh wave. Over the decades since the fifties, God has been at work in revival here in Argentina.

First Wave: The Tommy Hicks Campaign in the 1950s

A small group of missionaries had gathered together to pray. Though they had served the Lord faithfully and at great sacrifice, they were discouraged. It was then that one of them brought a forceful word, "Launch out into the deep and let your nets down for a draught." God was encouraging them to take steps of faith and to look beyond the lack of results. The census of the adult members of the Assemblies of God at that time was a total of only 174 in the entire nation.

It was in 1951 that God had brought a powerful visitation to a tiny group of students and faculty at River Plate Bible Institute (IBRP). One of their teachers, R. Edward Miller, was newly arrived on the mission field and filled with evangelistic zeal. During 1949, three missionaries had done an exhaustive census of the Christians in all three of the evangelical denominations that were doing some of the best work in the country. They came up with an astounding inclusive figure of only 574. Large churches numbered seven members. Discouraged at the lack of response to the gospel, R. Edward Miller wrote his sister, "I would do much better evangelizing in the United States."

Desperate for change, he began to pray. At the time, the Lord placed a heavy burden on his heart to see an awakening or a revival in the country. The beginnings of the answer from God came in the province of Mendoza on the Chilean border. God miraculously transformed the lives of six young men who had gone to disrupt the services of the revival. They ended up on the floor—knocked off their feet by the power of God. All of them decided to study at River Plate Bible Institute in Buenos Aires. "The teachers were just as bored as the students with the notes they were dictating in class," said Miller.

The training center had started with only twelve students in 1948 and had moved from the center of Buenos Aires to City Bell, sixty kilometers south, by 1951. One night that very year, a young student still in his teens had gone outside in a nearby field to pray. As Alexander was calling out to God well after midnight, he sensed a being from heaven. Terrified, he ran for the institute building, only to find it locked. Someone finally heard him calling and let him in, but the heavenly visitor entered with him. All the students woke up and felt the holy presence, becoming afraid as well. The prayer that ensued was memorable. Alexander, a young Polish immigrant, gave messages in tongues and the interpretation was given to Celsio, a young native who was so frightened that he could not verbalize the messages, but finally wrote them down. One prayed around the world, though he knew little of geography, and named city after city by name in its own language. He said later that he felt like he was taken there, looked down on the city, interceded for it, and felt that God would visit that place before the end came. During the three months that followed this initial visitation, the angel kept returning. As the students prayed, a tremendous burden for the nation of Argentina came upon them. They began to weep and travail before God. Some of them leaned against the brick wall and wept so much that the tears coursed down the wall and made puddles around their feet. Also, various prophesies, tongues, and interpretations were given during these months, some concerning the future of the nation of Argentina. One of the words that came related to Eva Duarte Peron, also known as Evita, who at that time was perfectly well. The word indicated that the thunder of God's presence would fall upon her heart and she would tremble before the presence of God. As history played out, she went to an early death. Another word said that Argentina would hear the Word, and many would be converted.

When the few churches caught wind that the IBRP students were saying they had received the visitation of an angel and there were prophesies like this, the church people began to scoff and make fun. For more than two years the school was the butt of many jokes. It all seemed impossible in a country where so few were even evangelical Christians. But God was at work.

About this time an evangelist in Tallahassee, Florida, got a vision from God. He saw the continent of South America as a field filled with wheat. It was beautiful, golden grain that moved in waves with the wind. Suddenly the stalks of wheat were transformed into people who stood with their hands raised crying, "Come and help us. Come and help us." God gave him a word that within two years he would be involved in South America.

The first united campaign was being planned in the city of Buenos Aires in the year 1954. A well-known evangelist was contacted but did not sense that he was the person for the campaign. That was when the organizers extended the invitation to Tommy Hicks, the evangelist who had received the South American "Macedonian call."

He agreed and was on the plane making his way toward Argentina when he sensed strongly a word unknown to him, "Perón—Perón." He asked the flight attendant what that word meant, and she looked at him strangely, saying, "That is our president."

"I must go see President Perón," he thought. When he arrived in Buenos Aires the church leaders tried to dissuade him, believing that Hicks could never get a soccer stadium for twenty-five thousand like he wanted, let alone fill it. Up until this time, so few had been converted or healed. However, convinced of his mandate from God, Hicks went to the Rose House (government house) to see the president.

When Tommy Hicks asked for the interview, he was greeted by an armed guard. "What do you want?" the guard asked brusquely. As Tommy Hicks explained carefully that he wanted to hold a healing and salvation crusade, the guard became intrigued. "You mean God can heal? Can He heal me?" the man asked. "Give me your hand," Tommy Hicks said and prayed a simple prayer of faith. God healed the man instantly and suddenly the secretary exclaimed, "Come back tomorrow. I will take you to see the president."

President Perón listened to everything Hicks told him and was very curious upon hearing that God could heal today. Perón was experiencing a very bad skin disease, an eczema which no doctor had been able to heal. It was forcing the president into seclusion and he was frustrated. When Hicks prayed for him, he was healed and told his secretary to give the visitor whatever he needed. Hicks started by asking for the use of a large stadium and free access to the state-owned radio and newspaper, all of which he was given.

The campaign lasted fifty-two days. So many came to the Atlantic Stadium that they moved to the much larger Huracan Stadium seating one hundred eighty thousand people. People even camped out in the stadiums to ensure they got a seat the next day. During the campaign God did so many miracles of healing that people sent the sick from neighboring countries to be prayed for. At times the stadium would be so full that some of the needy could not get in. They would touch the stadium walls and be healed. Ambulances would arrive with people on stretchers, and these same people would walk out after the service, healed by the grace of God.

It is estimated that two million people heard the gospel in less than two months! God had fulfilled His promise. The last evening of the campaign over two hundred thousand people gathered to hear the evangelist and to see God's mighty acts.

A shipment of thousands of Bibles was sold immediately. There was so much fruit; so many souls all at once; so many years of sowing and sowing and suddenly, more harvest than the leadership could handle. The miracles of those days include a tremendous variety. One of the IBRP students was healed of sterility and now has five children. The blind exclaimed, "I can see!" The paralyzed left their wheelchairs, and the crippled waved their crutches above the crowd, exulting in God's healing power. People were brought in on stretchers, many in ambulances, and were healed at the crusade. One three-year-old boy had only walked with braces, but his mother removed them by faith and the boy started walking. His own doctor was so moved that he gave his life to Christ right then and there.

Some time before the campaign, missionary Louis Stokes had announced a work day at the church he was planting in the neighborhood of Flores in the federal capital. He said, "God is going to send tremendous growth, and we need your help to tear down the back wall to make room for all the people He will be sending."

People in the congregation just looked at each other and smiled. There were so few of them that two benches could accommodate them comfortably. But they acceded to his request and were there on that Saturday. When the campaign drew to a close, that church had to hold five services on Sundays to deal with the large number of new believers.

Louis Stokes' daily journal of the Tommy Hicks Campaign includes a telling comment: "A revival is not a time of normal living and working and thinking, but of constant adjusting of one's activities and strength to the present and pressing problems and possibilities."[4]

The first wave of revival broke a series of years of fruitlessness and frustration. Though there were no breakthroughs prior to the Tommy Hicks' crusades, many people before this had served well and worked hard. The sacrifice of those early pioneers was critical in setting the stage for what was to come.

Among those courageous sowers of precious seed was British Missionary Allen Gardiner, who lived about a century before the Hicks' meetings. Seven missionaries had set out in 1850 from the port of Liverpool for Tierra del Fuego in Southern Argentina. They had a heart to share the gospel with the people of this cold land where the fire had to be carried from island to island (hence the name Tierra del Fuego or Land of Fire).

They had not raised enough money to leave England fully stocked, but there were promises of a later shipment of food and supplies. Feeling the urgency to spread the Good News, Gardiner and his crew had left, trusting for a shipment of food to reach them at a particular spot along the Argentine coast later on. However, this never happened. As Gardiner and his men grew weaker and weaker from the lack of provisions and as he watched his colleagues die of starvation one at a time, he wrote the following prophetic prayer as the last entry in his diary on September 3, 1851:

> I trust poor Fuegia and South America will not be abandoned. The missionary seed has been sown there, and the Gospel message ought to follow.[5]

His life became a seed planted in Southern Argentina, now Patagonia, and his subsequent dramatic death of starvation in that land became a clarion challenge that touched the hearts of many. Surely this sacrifice is a portion of the strong base for blessing and revival in our time.

Some of these later missionary pioneers had to bury their dead on the side of the road because only those of the official religion had access to the cemeteries. The work was very difficult, but God honors faithfulness. Praying for days and days, weeping and interceding, was not easy either, but God answered with an amazing manifestation of His power. With the Hicks campaigns, things broke open for the gospel in this land. The Pentecostal churches began to grow. Many of the present leaders came to Christ directly or indirectly because of Tommy Hicks' vision and obedience.

The tragic aspect of those unprecedented days is that there were not enough workers prepared to contain the harvest. The leaders God raised up became very aware that evangelistic campaigns are not just to bring in a lot of people. The people must then be consolidated and discipled or the fruit is lost.

WAVE OF THE 1960S: LORNE FOX

In the sixties, there was a beautiful move of God through the ministry of Lorne Fox. It was then that the manifestation of people falling under the power of God was seen by many for the first time. When the evangelist prayed, people would fall to the ground and later get up totally healed of things like paralysis and mononucleosis. Many conversions were reported. This was another wave of the previous campaign.

WAVES OF THE 1970S

During the seventies, various waves occurred including one initiated by Juan Carlos Ortiz who taught much on discipleship and was innovative in his approach to evangelism. During summer he had his congregation meet in the plaza to be more in touch with the unconverted people. Pastor Ortiz was ahead of his time and not always understood by the rest of the Pentecostal leadership.

Other waves of this decade include the ministry of Domingo Colihuinca Navarro, an evangelist of Araucanian origin used mightily of God in healings and even in resurrections. He planted approximately one hundred churches in his lifetime. In some of the towns where the train he was riding passed through, crowds of people blocked the tracks, asking him to stay and minister in their community. Brother Colihuinca recently ministered at IBRP. He is one hundred five years old and still full of God's fire. We had the honor of photographing him with a group of students who have determined to carry on the flame.

The charismatic renewal touched Argentina during the seventies and began to break down some of the rigid structures that were prevalent, especially concerning worship and liturgy styles.

A tremendous ministry that had its start during these years is that of Omar and Marfa Cabrera. They traveled the country in a healing and evangelistic ministry, opening meeting centers that some estimate reached more than fifty thousand in total attendance around the country. This was during a period when a congregation of one hundred twenty members was considered a large church.

WAVE OF THE 1980S: CARLOS ANNACONDIA CAMPAIGNS

Then came the economic crisis, and many had their personal hopes dashed. This was exacerbated by the tremendous loss of face brought on by the defeat of the Malvinas (Falklands) War. A proud and noble people found itself in a conflict that military leaders had chosen because they hoped that the population would thereby be distracted from the internal problems of the nation.

In this difficult time of desperation God raised up Evangelist Carlos Annacondia. Considering the uncertainty of the years of political dictatorship, the economic disaster, and the social and ethical fiber of the nation being shredded piece by piece, the church was doing well to survive and make some attempts at reaching out. No one dreamed of open fields filled with up to one hundred thousand people breathing in the hope of the gospel. No one except God. Who could imagine 931 sinners running forward at one time on one single night in a campaign? He is the verb that sends the power which causes the wave that then brings in the sediment. Thankfully, His servants were available and yielded. Pastors of various churches united, and Evangelist Annacondia preached and prayed night after night for up to sixty nights at a time, and God shook the nation for His glory.

The fruit of those campaigns was enormous. Today I spoke with a pastor who came to Christ in a Carlos Annacondia campaign in the city of Rosario. He had fled there to avoid being punished by his fianceé's family for having broken his engagement. At seventeen years of age he was running his own informal brothel of four women, including his own sister. He had purchased a house and was doing very well. But he was desperate for God to change him. He said to the Lord, "If you do something, the rest of my life belongs to you." When God touched his life that night, he walked into a bar and began to yell to the people that Jesus was real. When he returned to his city, he won his whole family to Christ; seven brothers and sisters and their spouses, his mother, and now his nineteen nieces and nephews belong to Christ.

Waves of the 1990s: The Anointing

It was in 1993 that pastor and national superintendent of the Assemblies of God, José Manuel Carlos was having his devotions. As he knelt that morning in prayer he was struggling to stay awake when the Lord gave him a vision. In it people were lined up in the street for blocks trying to get into church. Soon after, the vision's fulfillment became reality. Claudio Freidzon's church had up to four blocks of people standing in line trying to get in. The same began to happen at Pastor Osvaldo Carníval's, Pastor Hugo Weiss's, and Pastor Omar Olier's churches. People stayed for hours worshiping and receiving from God; enjoying Him.

During that time Marcos Witt's contemporary style of music combined perfectly with the strong emphasis on worship that was occurring in churches across the nation. Instead of testimonial choruses or doctrinal hymns, these were songs expressed directly to God in a fresh and new way that struck a chord throughout the church.

Another wave at that time came through the ministry of Sergio Scataglini with his powerful focus on the fire of God and holiness. His preaching led thousands to get their lives straightened out.

PRESENT WAVE: MULTIPLICATION

The present wave of revival has to do with reaching the lost through cell groups. These groups touch people wherever they are and work quickly to bring them to maturity. In the weekend encounters some new believers are brought to decisions that lead to inner healing and forgiveness, the baptism of the Holy Spirit, and commitment to service. Churches have doubled, quadrupled, and even grown tenfold with this new dynamic, coupled with the power of God.

A poignant moment was listening to Pastor Alberto Scataglini talk about the early days when the Carlos Annacondia evangelistic crusade was producing so much fruit. With a couple of tears running down his face and a choked up voice he said, "We just weren't ready for it. We lost so many people because we were not prepared to do follow-up."

The churches in Argentina now have organized to help new converts grow. They produce disciples who then become leaders that are prepared to go out and reproduce themselves.

Pastor Edgardo Muñoz states that true revival is when there is a commitment to the Great Commission. It is amazing to observe how God's powerful moving here is affecting many other nations. This is also part of the present move and the wave that seems to be swelling again for a fresh outpouring.

God's move in Argentina has been for the good of many. He never intended to bless a church or a nation merely to have the glory stagnate. "The wind bloweth where it listeth" (John 3:8), and the Spirit's character is the flowing of life towards those in need. If we do not share what we have received, especially for the sake of evangelizing the lost, God will cut the power, and we will be left only with a few anecdotes of yesteryear and a wistful confusion as to why God does not work in the same way anymore.

Many leaders in the revival have gone to other countries where God has done tremendous things. Pastor-evangelist Claudio Freidzon has been traveling to different countries of the world almost every week since 1993 when the powerful move of God broke out. Sergio Scataglini and Carlos Annacondia have also been traveling extensively, preaching and ministering in the power of the Holy Spirit. Wherever Carlos Annacondia goes in the world, people who manifest demons and are set free. This includes the poverty-stricken who are into witchcraft along with the well-dressed who seem to have it all together. The Breakthrough Conferences have been held around the world, including Malaysia, the U. S., and Europe. Dante Gebel has been involved in huge youth campaigns all across Latin America. Lesser known evangelists have also had an amazing impact in other nations. A critical fruit of revival is a passion for missions. Thank God much has been happening in this respect in Argentina, although there is a great deal of room to grow.

The Argentine National Missions Department, under the able leadership of Argentine pastors and missionary Brad Walz, has sent out and supported 179 missionaries to thirty-eight other countries since 1986. Here are a few stories of how the fire of the Argentine revival is affecting other countries.

A Student in Europe

Eliana Nervegna, twenty-three years old and a recent graduate of River Plate Bible Institute, had traveled to the Czech Republic with her father, evangelist Pablo Nervegna, to participate in a pastors' conference. To their surprise, they were informed at the border that they needed a visa to go into the country. After two days in Austria, they were able to obtain the necessary documentation.

When they arrived at the conference, they found out that the pastors who had been invited to speak had also been detained at the border for lack of a visa. To fill in some of the time until the slated speakers arrived, the organizers asked Eliana to speak one morning. In a country where it is not very common for women to preach and sacrificial offerings have not been taught, God led her to speak on stewardship. At the end of her message she led in the taking of an offering. The Holy Spirit told her to give the gold chain she had on in the offering, then to remove her shoes and give them, and her watch. Suddenly, the people went forward to give what they had. This went on for more than an hour. People would give the offering, go back to their seats to worship, and in a few minutes go forward to give again. Eliana later received a pair of new shoes and a watch. Many of those who had given so generously received financial miracles in their lives after that day.

The speakers had arrived, but the pastors all wanted Eliana to speak for the final evening, despite her insistence to the contrary. She had a glass of water in her left hand during the preaching since there was nothing to set it on. At the end of the message, the Holy Spirit impressed her to throw the glass of water on the crowd. She initially resisted, but finally gave in. The people who were so unceremoniously doused received the baptism in the Spirit and began to speak in tongues. Then God showed her a bottle of water off to one side of the platform. You guessed it, she started throwing water from the bottle! Thirty young people received the baptism in the Holy Spirit that day.

In Italy, a spirit of weeping came over the congregation when she spoke there. In New Jersey (USA) the same thing happened in one church, and, in another, twenty-five people received the baptism of the Holy Spirit.

Great Britain

"We'd like to do some friendship evangelism here in the neighborhood," they told Nomar and Andrea Banffi and Esteban Barbieri, a young Bible College student from Rey de Reyes Church in Buenos Aires who had gone over to Europe to attend a wedding. "Do you want to play soccer with us and the kids in the park?" they asked.

"We'd rather read a portion of the Bible to them and give a short testimony," they answered. This seemed like a very risky proposition, but the young people went along with it.

Esteban shared a brief testimony and then presented this challenge: "If you want to know if God is real," Esteban said to the soccer players, "let us pray for you." Most of them ran off and were laughing, but three who had listened the least walked over with a rather defiant attitude. As Andrea prayed, the three teenagers fell down on the blacktop! One of them lay there for over thirty minutes. The other two got up and asked for more. They explained that this was not a game and began to talk to them about committing their lives to the Lord. Twenty or thirty others crowded around wanting to feel God's power, too. Soon there were various young people strewn out on the ground. Some of them were only six years old.

One of their mothers ran over from an apartment building and tried in vain to get her son to stand up. "What did you do to him?" she wailed desperately. Soon, the police were called in. Just as the paddy wagon arrived to take the evangelists away, Esteban and his friends were leaving the park.

Those young boys will never wonder anymore if God is for real!

WALES

The cleaning lady came early to the church that had been used the evening before by Conrad Lampan, an Argentine evangelist who was visiting Wales. She was not able to do her work—because she kept falling over. *I wonder what went on last night,* she thought as she lay on the floor for a couple of hours.

Recently, Pastor Pablo Silberbeib and Argentine missionary Rocco DiTrolio ministered in Wales. How their hearts ached as they realized that the beautiful church buildings they saw everywhere had been transformed into gymnasiums or restaurants. The law does not allow the new owners to touch the exterior, so that the great spiritual heritage can be remembered, at least symbolically.

God used the two pastors from Argentina tremendously to bring pastors together for prayer in brokenness before Him. These people who have experienced eighteen major revivals are in dire need of another one, especially among the youth.

AFRICA: MOZAMBIQUE

In 1990, Walter Llanos was called to be a missionary to Mozambique while he was sitting in his dormitory room at River Plate Bible Institute. At the time, the country was under communist rule, and the only foreigners allowed in as residents were those that would be involved in social help, so he started school in pre-med.

In 1995 he decided to take a brief reconnaissance trip to Mozambique, along with forty other Argentine pastors and workers. One day they came to a church that had a cross with a little red rag hanging on it. During the service, the seventy members and their pastors manifested demons. Walter and the other visitors prayed for these people, and they were delivered. Later, they informed Walter that the pastor also doubled as a witch doctor. God had brought teaching and freedom to a situation of syncretistic deception. Later, he and his wife, Laura, went to Mozambique as missionaries. They have many stories related to the areas dominated by witch doctors, which include cobra snakes attacking their tires and the lights of their vehicle going out strangely as they crossed a 150-foot, one-lane, wooden bridge stretched out high above a river. The lights came back on after prayer. God has given them many wonderful testimonies of His care and protection, and they have been effective in that region.

BOLIVIA

This unique nation to the north of Argentina has had its own powerful visitation from God in the last few years. Evangelist Carlos Annacondia spent a few weeks in Cochabamba, Bolivia, and, according to pastors there, the reticence and resistance broke at that time, with a great deal of growth being experienced since then. In the second largest city of Santa Cruz, when Carlos Annacondia held a campaign there for three weeks, thirty thousand people made decisions of faith during that time.

Pastor David Vargas, a graduate of River Plate Bible Institute, has been working in the Cochabamba area for twenty-one years. Much of the political unrest in Bolivia during the last few years has started in this region. An independent, closed spirit was the norm among the population at large and also among the churches. But after Brother Carlos Annacondia's campaign in this city of 800,000, they began to experience a totally new atmosphere spiritually. Pastor Vargas states that during the twenty-five-day united campaign with evangelist Annacondia, "We closed the churches every night. Cochabamba was such a resistant place that it was called the 'tomb of missionaries.'" But God used Evangelist Carlos Annacondia to break spiritual strongholds. It was once impossible for a church to grow to any real size. Now there are various large churches of more than one thousand members."

Presently, there is openness and availability, a willingness to praise God and serve others. "More than anything, the Annacondia crusade awakened spiritual hunger in the city," Vargas continues. "We changed our molds for worshiping God from accordions and drums to something totally new because of the flow of the Spirit." Pastor Vargas's church has grown from two hundred to more than two thousand in these brief years since the Annacondia campaign.

THE UNITED STATES

Can you imagine someone preaching to a person in their car at a stoplight? That is exactly what Damián Gonzalez and North Central University students did one day on a busy street of Minneapolis. The first car put on its flashers and the driver just waved the cars behind to go ahead. The driver wanted to hear what was being said. Soon a whole line of vehicles had their flashers on and each driver was listening to his own personal evangelist. Boldness and a little God-centered lunacy at work!

More than one hundred fifty students went street-witnessing with Damián over a period of six weeks. Many people received Christ on the streets. One North Central University student even courageously prayed for a man on crutches, and his leg was healed. Several other students prayed for a sick little girl in a stroller with a very bad ear infection. The students noted that matter was seeping from the child's ear and asked the mother if they could pray. They happened to run across the mother later than same day, and the child was eating for the first time in days, feeling just fine.

Damián´s attitude when he arrived in Minnesota is demonstrated by this statement: "I didn't come here to bring the fire from Argentina. I came to work at your side and prove together the power of God that is here."

Another city that has been especially touched by our Lord is Miami. In fact, after a recent crusade at the Orange Bowl Stadium, the mayor of Miami handed over the key of the city to Evangelist Claudio Freidzon, certainly a symbolic honor.

The Breakthrough Conferences that have been held in the United States have also made an impact. In Cedar Rapids, Iowa; Minneapolis, Minnesota; and other cities across the U. S., these conferences preached by the Argentine revivalists and evangelists have resulted in the same kinds of miraculous healings, deliverance, and testimonies as here in Argentina.

WRAP-UP

These are just a few of the testimonies of the effects of God's powerful move beyond the boundaries of Argentina. It is evident that the key so often is bold faith that listens to God and does His bidding. The Lord uses that which is not, to confound and challenge the powers that be.

We are thankful for the 179 missionaries sent from the National Missions Department and serving in thirty-eight different countries. The total from all groups working in other cultures and nations at present is five hundred, which is admirable considering the economic crisis we have lived in for years.

God has been working for a long time in this country. Argentina has been open to what God wants to do, and it has impacted others in return. One of the greatest advocates for Argentine missionaries is Evangelist Carlos Annacondia. So much happened when this humble servant of God came on the scene.

3

A Harvest of Surprises

ONE OF THE most amazing waves of revival that has occurred in Argentina is the one that started in the eighties. This wave was a huge one, spreading out from La Plata and realizing the salvation of thousands of people. The key personalities in this wave included Pastor Alberto Scataglini in La Plata and the young evangelist Carlos Annacondia, newly converted businessman with some creative ideas. What followed brought not only a harvest of people, but also a harvest of surprises.

ALBERTO SCATAGLINI:
GOD PREPARES IN LA PLATA

La Plata is the capital of the province of Buenos Aires, the most populous and richest province of Argentina. Of the thirty-seven million inhabitants in Argentina, twenty-five million live in this province.

The city of La Plata is just south of the metropolis of Buenos Aires, and it is the center of many governmental activities and home to the Cathedral of La Plata. It is also the location of the National University of La Plata with an enrollment of 94,283 students.[1] A city strong in tradition, it is proud and was very resistant to the gospel. Masonic influence and atheism are strongly ingrained in the city.

Pastor Alberto Scataglini and his wife, Isabel, had taken the pastorate in La Plata when only fifty members were attending. Growth came very slowly. At this time evangelism rarely worked, but even those methods that worked somewhat in other areas of the country produced no results in this resistant city. For years the congregation had evangelized in the plazas of La Plata using music, films, and preaching, but it didn't seem to matter which technique was used, no fruit was forthcoming. They had been pastoring in La Plata for fifteen years when God prepared the scene for the tremendous revival that would sweep the nation and affect generations of believers.

The young people of the church talked with their pastor about their intense desire to commit to God's purposes. He in turn gathered the entire youth group and asked how many were willing to seek God earnestly and pay the price to see God work in their church and community. Of the fifty or sixty young people present, only six decided to make the commitment. Pastor Scataglini and these youth began praying in the church basement. When adult members of the congregation asked what was happening, the group involved gave vague answers because there was cohesion in the group at the time that they wanted to protect.

For months they prayed, and initially God placed on their hearts a very strong sense of conviction of sin. They began to weep and to confess their sins one to another. God spoke to them that the year be dedicated to consolidation and that the next year, 1984, would be conquest. By the end of the year the youth group had grown to two hundred in attendance, and Pastor Scataglini's idea was to send them out to start thirty different preaching points around the city.

I was invited to speak to the church leaders in 1983. Sergio Scataglini, Pastor Alberto's son, was working with them. Sergio had recently graduated from Fuller Theological

Seminary. During the day I spent with them I listened with some skepticism to the goals for the coming five years. The leadership of a church that was running five hundred was talking about reaching a goal of five thousand within five years. "Church growth formulas," I thought to myself. None of us could imagine that in a year the church would be running not just five thousand, but twenty thousand that would be visiting the mother church each month, and thousands more would be attending in three hundred different locations of the city of La Plata.

Pastor Alberto Scataglini recalls that at this time he found himself prophesying in the middle of a sermon and what came out of his mouth surprised even him. He said, "Some of you have sat in the same pew for years, and you are not interested in church growth. Either change or you will lose your seat. Not only will you lose your seat, but your place of ministry in the church." Some people's reaction was to laugh the warning off, but in just a little while, this is exactly what happened. The new converts would demonstrate more maturity and commitment than some believers with twenty-five years of attendance in the church.

An Unknown Evangelist

At that time they did evangelism in the streets and in the parks but saw very few results. They would plan an outreach during a period of six months and have only about thirty people accept Christ. Representatives of an evangelist unknown to Pastor Alberto Scataglini had contacted him various times because they wanted the church to participate in a united campaign that was being planned in La Plata. "When I asked how long this man had known the Lord, they answered, 'four years,'" said Alberto. "Then I asked if he had received theological training, and they said he had not. So I told them, no, we were not interested."

This unknown evangelist was Carlos Annacondia, and he went to Pastor Scataglini in person. As he sat on the couch in the pastor's home, God spoke to Alberto's heart and said, "Participate in the campaign, and do everything he says. This is My servant." So Pastor Scataglini agreed to participate.

"How do you think we should go about it?" asked Annacondia. Brother Scataglini was a recognized leader among the pastors, not only of the city of La Plata, but of the nation. He had held executive positions, including the office of national superintendent with the Assemblies of God of Argentina and was a very respected man with a great deal of experience.

"I am Elisha, and you are Elijah," Alberto said with humility. "You tell us. You are the evangelist, and we will do as you say," he continued, amazed at what was coming out of his mouth in this conversation with an untried evangelist. "When do we start the meetings?" asked Alberto.

"In two weeks," was the answer. This left the pastor incredulous. Six months would have been the minimum to plan a local campaign. Two weeks to get ready for an evangelistic effort that would involve all of the evangelical churches of La Plata seemed completely unrealistic. The organization and advertising it would require could not be accomplished in that time. But Pastor Scataglini swallowed hard. "All right," he said. "And where are you going to hold this?"

"In a tent in a field," the new evangelist said. Pastor Scataglini started to argue in his head that people would never come to a tent outside the city; not in La Plata. He thought of all the evangelistic tools they had used, none of which had worked. Why would people respond to something like coming to a tent in a field? But verbally he agreed.

The tent they did set up in the preliminary campaign north of La Plata in City Bell was all in tatters, but the preaching was done in front of it. To the consternation of the pastors, the tent was to be used to pray for deliverance. "That first night when Evangelist Annacondia gave the altar call, 144 people came forward to accept Christ. It seemed impossible. This was a very resistant city. Previously, we had put together evangelistic operatives where only one person was the result, a drunken man who came only because he could not see too well," recalls Pastor Alberto Scataglini.

THE TENT CRUSADE

The first site chosen in the city of La Plata was at the northern tip of the city by the river, near the area dominated by witches and warlocks. The crowds had swollen to the thousands, and many each evening were receiving deliverance in the "intensive care" tent. That name was invented by a student of Instituto Bíblico Río de la Plata. Both Pastor Scataglini and Evangelist Annacondia recall with gratitude that one hundred students helped out at the campaign every weekend for months.

As the event began, the noise level from the PA system was a little much for the neighbors who promptly called the police station and asked the chief of police to send someone down to control the situation.

Brother Alberto laughed as he stated that the first two policemen did not come back. So the chief of police sent two more. Those did not return either. So he sent even two more. When those did not return, he went to the campaign to see for himself what was happening and found his police officers being prayed for in the intensive care tent. The authorities determined then to put up with the neighbors' complaints and let the meetings go forward.

Pastor Alberto shares that it got so he didn't even undress. Someone was always coming in the middle of the night, asking for healing or bringing a person who was demon-possessed. So he and his wife just decided it was easier if he stayed dressed and ready. So many people were lined up to see him outside the church that he would climb into their apartment through an indirect way up a fire escape and through a window.

"One night they rang the doorbell, asking me to come down to the street to pray for a man," Scataglini recalled. "I told them to bring him up here but they said they couldn't because he had to be bound in the backseat he was so crazy. I went down to the car and prayed for this man who was literally raving in his chains. The demons left him. This kind of thing happened often."

Before the evangelistic crusade began, one of the goals that Scataglini had set with his church leadership included opening thirty preaching points that year. It was a very ambitious and worthy goal. But God multiplied the results by ten. At the end of the year, the church had opened three hundred preaching points all over the city!

The totality of the La Plata campaign in 1984 was eight months duration. The results were astounding: fifty thousand decisions for Christ.

CARLOS ANNACONDIA:
THE EVANGELIST'S BEGINNINGS

In the years preceding the La Plata crusade, 1983–1984, Argentina was coming to "the age of failure of nerve" with the "dirty war" struggle against guerrillas that was causing a state of near anarchy. The economy was also in shambles, at times hitting five thousand percent inflation per year. On top of that was the loss of the Falklands War (Islas Malvinas) to Great Britain. The Argentines had been told they were winning. A proud people, the nation was shocked and humiliated when they found out that they had lost.

During this time, God was rescuing an agnostic businessman with nine children who owned his own nuts and bolts factory and had a weekend home.

"The day we were converted, everyone in my family, including my wife, María, was baptized in the Holy Spirit except me," Carlos recalls. He heard someone who had also been filled with the Spirit, speaking in tongues and singing in perfect English, "When the Saints Go Marching In." The believer who was singing didn't speak very good Spanish, but his singing in English was perfect.

"In the Spirit my wife would sing a lyric sound that was just beautiful," recalls Carlos. "So I said to God, 'Baptize me in the Spirit, or I'm going to die.' When I received the baptism in the Holy Spirit I started yelling in tongues for ten hours. It changed my voice. I've never had the same voice. I left there and would talk to people in what I thought in my mind was Spanish, but it actually was in tongues."

One night he heard the pastor preach from Mark 16:17–18: "And these signs shall follow them that believe; In my name shall they cast out devils; they shall speak with new tongues; They shall take up serpents; and if they drink any deadly thing, it shall not hurt them; they shall lay hands on the sick, and they shall recover." Carlos thought, *Where are the sick? In hospitals. I'll go pray at the hospital.* So he took one of his children with him and headed to a hospital.

At the time, the country was under a military dictatorship, and there were guards posted at the entrance to the hospitals to avoid the loss of medicines to the terrorists. Carlos approached the guard and asked to go into the hospital to pray. The guard said that unauthorized entrance was forbidden. Holding his child in his arms, Carlos walked to the corner and prayed simply, "Lord, you know I want to do your bidding and heal the sick. Please make me invisible so I can go in there and pray for them." With that he walked up to the same guard and right past him. The guard never blinked.

He found himself in a ladies' ward with approximately forty women in one large room. One by one he asked if he could pray for them for healing. "I'm of another religion," they would answer him and refuse prayer. Finally, he walked up to the last bed where a fifteen-year-old girl lay paralyzed. He told her that the Lord wanted to heal her. As he spoke to her about Christ, she began to weep and accepted Him as Savior.

Then he heard the Lord say to him, "Tell her to get up. She's healed."

Carlos thought he should at least pray for her. After all, he had a special prayer prepared and wanted to use it.

The Lord reiterated, "She's healed. Tell her to get up." So he said, "Get down from your bed, the Lord has healed you." Since she didn't respond immediately, he pushed her out of bed, and she started to walk. Suddenly the girl was running down the aisle between the beds.

"Stop, you can't do that," the nurse yelled. "Who said you could walk? You're paralyzed. Get back into bed." But the girl kept walking down the aisle.

Suddenly all the ladies jumped down from their beds and walked toward him crying, "¡Pastor, ore por mí! (Pastor, pray for me.)" Some of them even approached, wheeling their plasma bottle holders. They forgot about religion when they saw the sign of God's power. Evangelist Annacondia smiles as he says, "I was one month old as a Christian and already they were calling me pastor." What a moment at the beginning of a trajectory of tremendous faith.

In the first months of his life in Christ, Carlos Annacondia began to devour the Word. For years a Bible someone had given him had sat on his bedroom lamp stand unopened. But now, each time he saw those pages, he was filled with faith to believe what he was reading.

It was when he was two months old as a Christian that God showed him the world as a globe. "Suddenly it became like gelatin and then it began to beat like a heart," Carlos said. "I could hear the cries and the moans of the people, and I said, 'What is this, Lord?'"

God answered, "The world is weeping and groaning and calling out."

Carlos said, "Lord, send me."

Then the Lord asked, "Are you willing to pay the price?"

And Carlos answered, "Yes, Lord."

Part of the price has been leaving his family for weeks on end. He works late into the nights, ministering to the needs of the people. Another portion of the cost is the many attacks, both physical and spiritual, on his person. Many times killers have tried to take his life, but he always rests in God's protection. Carlos even has people poke him in the back or grab his hands and place them on their heads or on someone else's head, seeking a blessing.

ARGENTINA WILL BE MINE

Something else the Lord spoke to his heart when he was such a new Christian seemed almost ludicrous at the time, "Soon, soon, Argentina will be mine."

When he shared this with his believing friends, they thought he was crazy. At that time, toward the beginning of the eighties, there were very few believers in Argentina. The Tommy Hicks healing services had affected mostly Buenos Aires, and much of the Pentecostal leadership and churches could trace their launching to those days. But years of plenty had led the country into complacency. A person could witness, and the answer was always, "That's interesting, but I'm of another religion, and my family would never understand if I wanted to change." Finding another believer, say, riding the subway in downtown Buenos Aires was the cause of a three-week celebration.

Churches were built to accommodate one hundred to one hundred fifty people. When the pastors were asked why they had built the churches so small, they would answer, "So the church will look full." Winning Argentina for Christ seemed out of the question. In Brazil faithful prayer warriors had been interceding for their neighboring country for years and were about to desist, thinking there would never be a break-through. So it is no wonder that other more seasoned and experienced Christians were condescending toward Carlos Annacondia as a new convert with his wild ideas about "Argentina soon belonging to God." But God knew whom He had chosen—a man of faith and simple obedience whose consuming passion from the beginning was souls.

In those early years of his evangelistic ministry, Brother Annacondia would speak wherever he found an opportunity. One campaign was being held in a large shed with a corrugated tin roof. As he was preaching, someone from across the avenue began to throw rocks on the roof. With no ceiling or insulation, the projectiles made a lot of noise as they ricocheted and rolled down the metal roof. Suddenly, half in human frustration, the evangelist stated forcefully, "The person who is throwing rocks will soon be here at this altar, kneeling and accepting Jesus." Soon the din of rocks falling was interrupted. The silence came as a surprise to everyone. In no time the man was shaking and kneeling at the front of the church, weeping as he accepted the Lord.

Later he told the leaders what had happened to him. When he had stooped over to throw the next rock, two hands had grabbed him by the shoulders and stood him up erect. He looked behind him, and there was no one to be seen. Those same hands pushed him toward the campaign building. In two more shoves he was across the avenue. A couple more shoves, and he was kneeling at the altar repenting of his sins! Angels do participate in evangelism.

God's Protection

Various stories from those early days of preaching were related to the evangelist by neighbors, eyewitnesses, or even the very perpetrators of mischief who later found themselves in the intensive care tent, repenting of their sins and being freed of demonic possession. These experiences have to do with God's protection of His servant.

One outreach was being held in a rough neighborhood with violent young men surrounding the site. As a joke, a gang of these men decided to turn the evangelist's car over. Each time they attempted to come near the car, they were thrown backwards on their posteriors. That prank never materialized.[2]

Juan Di Crescienzo, the coordinator of those early campaigns, shares two impacting testimonies:

> We were in a very dangerous neighborhood where there were various gangs. I was accompanying evangelist Carlos Annacondia one night, preparing to present him, when we heard two gunshots. One of the bullets hit Carlos Annacondia in the back of the neck—I saw it hit the one speaking—and it became flattened there. It fell on the wood floor and thorough a crevice onto the grass so when we looked for it later we could not find it.
>
> Another testimony during that campaign in the same place, Bernal Oeste: four or five gangs were there every night. They would cause disturbances and get drunk. As coordinator I had to keep order, so I shared with them until the early morning hours, listening to their complaints and their problems. Every night the *colaboradores* (volunteer workers) would give me the offering bags behind the platform where my car was parked. Once we had all of them, five or six brothers would accompany me to a place fifty meters away where a brother had loaned us a little wooden shack where we would count the offering. But one of those days I was surprised that the colaboradores did not come. They left me alone. I waited ten or fifteen minutes and watched as those gangs went by, all of them armed with revolvers, knives, machetes, and some sawed-off shotguns. They kept walking past me and did not greet me.

It gave me the impression that they did not see me.

I got tired of waiting, so I went walking those fifty metres to the little house. There I found that the brothers waiting were in fear as they had heard that the five gangs had agreed to rob the offering that night. I thank God for keeping me. Later I found out on the last night of the campaign that the leaders of three or four of the gangs told me they were going to rob me of the offering. But they said, "We looked for you but could not find you. But today we are remorseful. Look at us; we are not drunk anymore."

I told Carlos Annacondia what had happened, and before going up on the platform he began to pray and to reprove, and those fifteen or twenty people, approximately, fell under the power of God. We would pray for them, but there was no way to get them to react.

This was a very rough experience because we were in the beginnings of those first campaigns, and we did not have experience to be able to minister deliverance. It was something novel because we had not seen anything like this.

The gang members looked like worms all interlaced. After the meeting ended, Carlos prayed again for these people, and they were still fallen there on the ground. I finished as coordinator and started to take the platform apart. We lifted everything onto the truck, and they were still there on the ground. I spoke to them in the name of the Lord. Then I said, "Lord, here they are in Your hands. If there is judgement over them, please forgive them." And we left. Some pastors who were there observing stated that when they finally got up they didn't remember anything. We don't know what happened to them, but when God begins a work in a person He continues to perfect it.[3]

Where that wooden shack stood now a church has been built.

It was at those meetings that a young man was healed of a hernia. His mother returned the next night inexplicably to scoff and make fun. As she waited for the bus to go home she had a vision of a wheelchair and sensed God say to her, "This is what awaits you until the end of your days if you do not repent of your taunts." She fell to the ground paralyzed! Someone helped drag her back into the meetings. As the campaign workers took her over to Brother Annacondia, she was weeping and pleading, "God, forgive me. Please forgive me." When the evangelist prayed, God in His mercy returned this woman to health.

On another occasion some young men decided to have one of them act as if he was paralyzed and then make sport of the evangelist for praying for him. The amazing development was that the person "acting" in the wheelchair truly ended up paralyzed for about three hours until he received prayer and confessed everything.

Early Campaigns and Power Encounters

The first time Carlos Annacondia held an evangelistic outreach with various churches participating was in 1984 in City Bell, a community close to La Plata. At IBRP we heard stories of teeth being filled miraculously and felt very hesitant about such a testimony. The decision to go and check things out for ourselves was a stepping stone toward our students being involved nightly in the ministry at the next campaign in the city of La Plata.

It had been in the town of City Bell that IBRP students had prayed and wept for Argentina months previous to the Tommy Hicks meetings when God gave them such an amazing visitation. Now, City Bell was having a critical role again concerning the future of the nation.

As the effort in La Plata began to bring deliverance of demonic activity to thousands, the business of mediums, witches, and warlocks was being affected. In much the same way as the deliverance of the young woman soothsayer of Philippi affected her owners' pocketbook, these marketing experts of the spiritual world were being left without clientele. So one evening they determined to unite forces. Taking advantage of their potions that included the ashes of human corpses, they tried to blow the evangelist off the platform. There was a strong wind, but the evangelist preached anyway, and God brought healing, conversion, and deliverance that night as usual.

Some of the witches and warlocks included garments from their clients among those that were placed on tables to be prayed for. To their happy surprise, their customers recovered and the witches charged them accordingly. However, as time went on, most of these businesses had to close down because the people had now encountered the truth of Jesus Christ and had become aware of the deception being foisted on them by those who served the darkness. Even many of the witches gave up and placed a sign in their windows, "Closed. Gone to the campaign."

It was at a weekend service in the park in Lomas de Zamora that two psychologists showed up with other therapists and teachers. They were at the meetings to study unconventional forms of therapy and try to understand what was happening. Soon many of them were being healed. One of the psychologists surrendered his life to Christ that weekend and another fifteen days later. One began to work on Carlos Annacondia's team. He is Basilio Benitez, our son-in-law's father. He and his colleague began to witness to all of their former psychology clients and won many of them to Christ. Basilio's colleague, Guillermo Santos, served with him for years on a church staff and is now in Spain as a missionary of the Argentine Assemblies of God.

PRINCIPLE 1: Staying in a Place

The Lord led Evangelist Annacondia, his team of coworkers, and the pastors in a very definite way during those early campaigns. One of the aspects of the wisdom God gave them involved staying at a place long enough to really make a difference in the spiritual realm. The outreach efforts lasted two months or longer in a single location.

"There was spiritual warfare, a direct attack on Satan and his demonic entourage," the evangelist states. "The result was that the heavens were opened up, and people were healed and delivered. Many even came to the campaign site throughout the day to ask how they could accept Christ." When buses would pass the campaign site, sometimes the people riding them would manifest demons and fall to the floor of the bus.

"The anointing was on the place," says Carlos. "The longer we stayed in a place, the more the heavens would open, and God would move in that place." Much of this has to do with the vast amount of prayer that goes into the services.

Another testimony that sounds like portions of the Old Testament has to do with some young men who decided to play soccer on the open field that had been cleared so well and stamped down by thousands of people during the meetings held there. The campaign had recently moved to another location, but as these boys played on what was evidently holy ground, they would suddenly fall down under the power of God.

PRINCIPLE 2: A Large Ministry Team

Another clearly anointed concept came to Annacondia when he was new in Christ. He would watch people's hunger to be ministered to. When special speakers drove away from his church, the congregation would surround the car and try to connect with the evangelist, if only by touching the door or the windows of the car. He thought to himself, "Why can't everyone pray and participate?" As a young Christian, Carlos Annacondia determined that it was important for every person to have their needs ministered to and if he ever got a chance to be used of God, he would be sure to use others to pray so all the people who wanted ministry could receive it. When God began to use his life, he broadened the scope of those who ministered with him, allowing pastors and leaders to work alongside his team casting out demons and praying for people.

At the beginning of the La Plata outreach, which lasted eight months, all seven of the churches in La Plata participated. Pastor Alberto Scataglini's church was the largest of those congregations involved. Soon news of the many healings and deliverances was being carried in expanding waves from the epicenter of the campaign. With thousands attending the open-air meetings and hundreds accepting Christ each night, ushers, counselors, and intercessors were desperately needed.

The leadership of IBRP determined to send a bus each evening to help, especially in the deliverance tent. It was our students who came up with the new name for ushers: "stretcher-bearers." They were the ones that had learned to pick up a demon-possessed person who was writhing on the ground, growling and gnashing his teeth, and carry him or her to the tent to be prayed for in a more specific and personal way. Two stretcher-bearers at a time would lift the person from the ground and hike their hips into the middle and start running. The "intensive care tent" was where you received the best intensive care of the universe: the name of Jesus through the power of His blood. When the crowds swelled to one hundred thousand at a time, the determination early on to let others participate and minister became a crucial piece of the puzzle that the Lord was putting together to bless the entire nation.

There are so many who are willing to help here. When a call went out in those first campaigns for volunteers to set up the tent, four hundred to six hundred would show up, when only sixty were needed. More than three hundred had to be sent home with the promise that they could help out the next time.

PRINCIPLE 3: Prayer

There is enough space under the preaching platform for five hundred people to be in prayer at the same time during the entire service. Prayer was a critical aspect of the meetings, and they continued from seven o'clock when the first choruses were sung, through ten o'clock when the evangelist arrived, and on to one thirty when he finished praying for needs. In many united evangelistic efforts, one thousand would sign up to pray during the service. There were two shifts of five hundred, and these people missed all the colorful singing and ministry; they missed watching the demon-possessed fall and be freed by the power of God. Their role was prayer backing, and they took it very seriously.

In the Mar del Plata campaign there were only three hundred workers available at the beginning. Sixty days later, there were three thousand, of which two thousand seven hundred were new converts from the outreach. The San Isidro revival meetings had the participation of four hundred congregations. Most of the pastors who were involved cancelled services at their own church buildings for the thirty-day duration of the campaign, and everyone helped out.

PRINCIPLE 4: Ministering Discreetly and Meaningfully to Every Single One

Another critical aspect of that powerful move was Evangelist Annacondia's determination that no one who wanted prayer should leave without having been ministered to. Most nights he would pray for people until three o'clock. The attitude was not, "Annacondia must pray for me, or I won't leave." He was praying, accompanied by many of the participating pastors who were also staying on to minister to people until that late hour. How similar to the attitude Jesus showed, "When he saw the crowds, he had compassion on them, because they were...like sheep without a shepherd" (Matt. 9:36). The disposition to care for and value each person was part of the dynamic of the Holy Spirit that we all learned.

A related concern that was staunchly pursued by Annacondia was to protect the person's dignity. That was the reason for the intensive care tent. The idea was to get those who had fallen to the ground and were writhing around, out of the public view so as to avoid embarrassing them. Only pastors or trained leaders were allowed in the tent. This also guarded people from goggling eyes that could affect or interrupt the working of the Holy Spirit.

THE RIPPLE EFFECT

Another dynamic of those amazing evangelistic efforts was their long-term consistency. Rain or shine, the services would go on day after day. One time in the Haedo Campaign it was raining extremely hard, but the evangelist still preached and thousands of people stood with their umbrellas taking in the positive word of the gospel.

"Continuity also made it possible for the cloud of God's presence to descend on a place," states Brother Carlos. "In a three-day event there can be a lot of fruit. But it isn't the same as what happens when the meetings have gone on forty days or even sixty days."

It would be almost like a ripple effect when the event was longer. "The first wave of miracles affects those who are in a close radius to the campaign. They tell all their relatives and friends and the next circle is wider. Then all of those people tell their friends and within just a few days we would have one hundred thousand people show up."

No Dividing Lines

Carlos learned a lot about the location of the meetings as well. It is a very practical, loving, nuts-and-bolts approach to ministry, and it works. "If you hold the campaign in a stadium, there is a dividing line," the evangelist says. "If you hold it in a large theater, there is also a dividing line. You will only get a portion of the family since not everyone will want to cross that line because of inhibitions from years of tradition. If you hold it in an open field, preferably in a neighborhood setting, accompanied with a festive atmosphere, you will have the whole family walk up, and they have not crossed any line. They are just out for a walk. Entire families accept Christ in this way."

Another aspect of the open field location was that there was no limit to the growth that the campaign could sustain. In a way similar to George Whitefield's open air meetings which also grew to up to one hundred thousand in attendance, Annacondia's services were also set to affect many.

Carlos believes that the crusades being held near populated neighborhoods allowed the word to spread more quickly and to affect people more deeply. On the platform the family who just walked up would see the neighborhood butcher giving testimony concerning a healing or deliverance from alcoholism and the impact was powerful. This was a person known to them, so it added immediate credibility to the gospel.

A Festive Occasion With Great Results

As one approached the campaign site, there was a feeling of excitement in the air. Hundreds of people were walking toward the open field. Trucks and buses and cars would be in a near traffic jam to get close. Garlands of lights crossed the streets, causing a festive atmosphere. Dozens of *choripan* or sausage hotdog stands surrounded the area, along with popular and folkloric music, usually rapid-paced and including testimonial words.

We all knew when the evangelist was about to walk on the platform. The key song was "El Hombre de Galilea Va Pasando, va"[4] ("The Man of Galilee Is Passing By"). The center of the singing was Jesus. The center of Carlos Annacondia's speaking was Jesus. The power displayed belonged to Jesus!

Testimonies of healing and deliverance were taken just before the evangelist preached. A clear, concise, loving message was proclaimed, usually based on a miracle of Christ's in the gospels and peppered with true-life testimonies.

Then came the moments we were anxiously awaiting, the call to accept Christ, followed by the prayer for healing and needs and deliverance to bring down satanic power.

Hundreds of workers lined up holding a rope thirty yards in front of the large platform, looking out at the crowd during the entire service. Then Brother Annacondia would give the invitation and ask the volunteer workers to lower the rope and let people come forward to the platform area. Night after night, hundreds would run up in desperation, with their hands raised in surrender before Christ.

"I want to give you two presents tonight from Jesus," Carlos would state with such tenderness. "The first one is a hug from Him because He loves you, and the second is a kiss from Him to let you know how important you are to Him."

Then he would ask the coworkers to take people's names and addresses so they could receive follow-up from the participating churches. During this lapse of time, more choruses were sung, and we enjoyed music from special singers.

After we had waited for everyone who made a decision to be prayed with and to fill in the cards, Brother Carlos would begin to pray for the needs and insist that Satan loose those he had bound. "Oíme bien, Satanás, (Listen to me well, Satan)," he would cry out, and begin a combination prayer to God and spiritual warfare confrontation with the enemy. Suddenly dozens of people all over the crowd would start falling to the ground, writhing and growling or groaning. Many who fell just lay peacefully. Brother Carlos would instruct the ushers or stretcher-bearers to leave those alone and only carry to the intensive care tent those who were writhing.

After that time of prayer, he and the participating pastors would walk over to the large tables piled high with the clothing of those who did not come because of illness or other reasons. They would all pray with much conviction and mercy over those items, and the relatives and friends would then take them back to their affected loved ones. Myriad testimonies exist of healings, conversions and deliverances. Next the evangelist and the pastors would begin to pray for the sick or needy for as long as it took to give them each a personal time of ministry.

The results of those first campaigns are awe-inspiring. Actually, the jump in decisions from the beginning of Carlos' ministry to the La Plata meetings and those that followed is phenomenal.[5]

YEAR, PLACE, AND NUMBER OF PEOPLE WHO ACCEPTED CHRIST		
1981	Don Bosco (Beccar)	110
1982	Villa Domínico	100
1982	Florencio Varela (Alpargatas)	70
1982	Florencio Verela (Barrio San Eduardo)	279
1983	Quilmes (Kolynos)	700
1983	Don Bosco (Beccar)	1,000
1983	Ezpeleta	350
1983	Bernal (IAPI)	750
1983	Francisco Solano	700
1983	Quilmes Oeste	800
1983	Wilde	1,500
1983	Bosques	600
1983	Tres Arroyos	100
1984	Berisso	2,000
1984	Ranelagh	1,600
1984	City Bell	1,700
1984	La Plata, Ensenada and Tolosa	50,000
1984	Monte Grande	8,500
1984	Lomas de Zamora	1,800
1984	Mar del Plata	83,000
1985	San Justo	60,200
1985	San Martín	57,000
1985	Moreno	16,000

All of these campaigns took place in the province of Buenos Aires, where half the population of the country lives.

The duration of the La Plata campaign was eight months.

By contrast, in just one weekend, one thousand eight hundred people accepted Christ in Lomas de Zamora. In just forty days, eighty-three thousand made decisions in Mar del Plata.

When Evangelist Annacondia held a crusade in the city of Córdoba, seven hundred kilometers from the capital, fifty thousand people accepted Christ in fifty-three days.

At one service, I counted fifty people sitting in a large tree so they could see better. In another, I watched the entrance to the intensive care tent as the stretcher-bearers brought the demon-possessed in: seventy-three in ten minutes! Students of IBRP have been present when seven hundred people manifested demons all at once. Brother Carlos says there were times that even one thousand were manifesting. This is when the large team composed of hundreds of pastors and leaders was essential in helping to pray for people.

Some Stories

One of the more comical testimonies of the evangelistic outreaches involves a man who had told his wife he would not go to the meetings; she could go ahead, but he accompanied her only to within ten blocks of the site. "People are diving on the ground," he said. "I don't want anything to do with it." The idea he had was that everything was prepared to impress or manipulate people. He could hear the PA system even ten blocks away, as he stood next to his car with his little dog standing on the hood of his car. Carlos Annacondia was praying and saying, as he did most nights, "Don't worry about those who are falling. Toca, Señor, toca (Touch, Lord, touch)." He had no sooner said those words than the little dog fell down on the hood of the car with his legs sticking straight up in the air.

The man stared at his dog in disbelief and must have thought, "This dog is more open to God than I am." He grabbed the little pet and ran toward the altar with his hands raised to accept Christ.

Another comical incident took place when Brother Carlos held meetings in Santiago del Estero. The powers that be in that town determined that they would come against the evangelistic effort with a religious procession. So they found an image and marched toward the campaign site holding it high. As they walked up to the entrance, the procession participants fell to the ground, including their image.

I was sharing this testimony in class and was pleased to hear from a young lady who said that many of the people who participated in that procession are now faithful leaders in her church!

Other Changes Brought by the Revival

During those days of the campaigns, suddenly every church tried to purchase a tent to have its own outreach. Since pastors and leaders had already been used of God in authority to heal or cast out demons, the power of God was made available all over the country in neighborhood evangelistic meetings.

Non-resident Bible Institutes began to proliferate all over the country. From eight Bible schools with an attendance of 180 in all, the numbers grew to a total of 5,500 in ministerial training in just eight years. The resident Bible Institute, IBRP, grew from eighty students to 342 in just seven years. An extensive training program called IETE (Instituto de Educación Teológica) was begun. Two other resident schools were also started during this time.

Within three years, the revival had caused major growth crises in Pentecostal training centers. A non-denominational training program called Seminario Biblico de Fe grew to hundreds of students only five years after the La Plata outreach. Training has been critical in maintaining the fruit of the revival.

An amazing aspect of the revival has been God's move among the prisons. In 1983 Pastor Juan Zuccarelli began his work in the jails in Unit 1 of Olmos with only four inmates that knew the Lord. The next year he was led by God to train as a guard to be able to pastor these men behind bars. From those small beginnings there are now 8,000 inmates in the Province of Buenos Aires who have accepted the Lord, and through this ministry a total of approximately 30,000 prisoners have accepted Christ. There is even one entire Christian jail dedicated to leaders among the inmates, Unit 25. This is the first jail in the world of purely Christian inmates. Obviously, these men have received Christ once they were behind bars.

Today both IBRP and the Christian and Missionary Alliance's Instituto Bíblico Buenos Aires are sending teachers weekly to train Christian leaders of the jail churches.[6]

SERGIO SCATAGLINI

The young Bible School student from IBRP was preaching on the street corner and gave the call to accept Christ. People in the high-rise apartments across from the park were raising their hands to signify that they were surrendering their lives to the Lord.

Years before, his mother, Isabel, had seen a vision of her son which included the flags of many countries. She wondered what it meant and how to receive it, and then an utterance in tongues and interpretation came in the service. "This is of me. Receive it because I will fulfill what I have promised."

Sergio, son of Pastor Alberto Scataglini, was mightily touched by God in Argentina and in the U. S. His ministry of fire has touched the world. He has a radio program that reaches twenty countries and he personally visited and ministered in thirty-five nations; also his two books have been translated into at least twelve languages. Together with his wife, they currently hold services on their Internet church, and have people from fifteen different nations connected. They are planting cells and have a school of leaders online.[7]

One day he was about to greet a church in Indiana and then drive quickly over to another church to preach. God had laid it on His heart to bring together as many pastors as possible to pray for the city. As he was about to speak, he fell down shaking behind the pulpit. He had to be carried out to his car but could not drive to the other church. A friend drove him to his in-law's home, where he and his wife were staying, and he had to crawl up the stairs to the bedroom. The experience lasted four days and deeply changed his life and ministry. The Lord spoke to him and said, "It is not enough to be 99 percent holy. It must be 100 percent." One percent poison can ruin the other 99 percent of a glass of water. Traveling between the U. S. and the church in La Plata, God began to demonstrate his fire more and more.

Breakthrough Conferences

Though Sergio Scataglini and his wife, Kathy, have a widespread and well-known ministry, they often have teamed up with Carlos Annacondia and Claudio and Betty Freidzon to hold events called Breakthrough Conferences. The Holy Spirit gave the vision to hold these renewal conferences to missionary Don Exley. His burden was for pastors and missionaries around Latin America and from the U. S. and other countries to experience the revival that has been going on in Argentina. Once again the dynamic of the Spirit is evident: team ministry by anointed evangelists and pastors who work together in a symphony of fire, power, and love.

Hundreds of pastors and missionaries have had their lives and ministries transformed by these events. Services and teaching times are held morning, afternoon, and night. During the time of ministry at the altar, leaders from Brazil, Great Britain, Mexico, Chile, Paraguay, and so many other places run to the altars seeking more from God.

One of the couples deeply affected by these conferences has

been the Ambassador from Malaysia and his wife, His Excellency Dennis and Cherry Ignatius, Ambassador Extraordinary and Plenipotentiary. He was the Ambassador to Argentina for many years, and most recently has served in Canada. During the first breakthrough they attended, the Holy Spirit spoke to their hearts prophetically that He would be using them to open the door to Malaysia and other nations of Asia. A breakthrough and an evangelistic outreach have followed in that very challenging country. The attendance was large and thousands made decisions for Christ, piling into the altar space with arms raised and tears streaming down their faces. For the conference, there were also some 2,700 pastors and leaders from thirteen countries (Australia, Brunei, China including Hong Kong, Indonesia, India, Malaysia, Myanmar, Philippines, Russia, Singapore, Taiwan, Thailand, and the United States), representing more than 450 churches. Fourteen pastors came from the interior of China, traveling five days by train, boat, and plane to get to Kuala Lumpur. Breakthrough Conferences have also been held in the countries of Canada and Malaysia and in the states of Texas, Louisiana, Indiana, and California.

It was my privilege to translate for Sergio Scataglini and for Carlos Annacondia in Minneapolis at Emmanuel Christian Center. One of the evenings, the church had the most people in attendance in its forty-year history: 3,200. That evening, two witches were part of the audience; they had come to cause trouble. When Brother Annacondia prayed, they fell to the floor and were taken out to the gym, which doubled as an intensive care center. Drugs and cigarettes were thrown on the platform by those finding deliverance in one of the services. Many people testified of healing of nearsightedness, migraine headaches, spine problems, and cysts that disappeared. Each night the large platform was filled with people who came forward to testify that they had felt God's healing touch. One man even got up from his wheelchair and ran across the platform.

God is at work everywhere, and those early beginnings in that little tent in City Bell and La Plata were at the core of it.

Wrap-Up

God has a plan for Argentina, and He has brought together many key players for the task. Thankfully they have been available to Him, holding nothing back and being generous with their personal time and energy. They have also been willing to work together and to allow others to participate. Their desire is to seek God with all their hearts, and they have taught so many of us that "as it is written, Eye hath not seen, nor ear heard, neither have entered into the heart of man, the things which God hath prepared for them that love him" (1 Cor. 2:9).

This wave of revival in the eighties prepared the way for God to spread the revival even further. The pastors who emerged out of this time grew into strong leaders who were to have some surprises of their own.

4

Leading Pastors

A N EVIDENT BYPRODUCT of the revival has been the growth of many congregations, often to over a thousand in attendance. In a country where only fifty years ago a large evangelical church had six or eight members, it is amazing to see the many large churches that have come out of this revival. A recent publication placed the Assemblies of God churches in Argentina at a million people, easily the largest denomination in the country now. Many estimate the total evangelical population at three million.

The general church attendance of the following pastors adds up to a lot of souls: Pedro Ibarra—eight thousand; Claudio Freidzon—twelve thousand; Osvaldo Carnival—twenty thousand; Guillermo Prein—thirty-one thousand; Omar Olier—eight thousand; Norberto Carlini—over three thousand, along with churches of one to two thousand for Moisés Barrientos, Héctor Ferreyra, Edgardo Muñoz, Pablo Deiros, Bernardo Stamateas, Alberto Aranda, Don Exley, Enrique Strohschein, Alberto Scataglini, Omar Olier, and Alberto Rey.

There are so many pastors who have been leaders in this move of God. The revival is not composed of just a few supergiants, but rather is inherent in a broad spectrum of people and churches. However, there is no doubt that certain names are easily recognizable. Their stories, impact, and testimonies keep bubbling to the surface in any telling of the revival in Argentina. Osvaldo Carníval, Guillermo Prein, and Claudio Freidzons are pastors who would be listed as leaders by almost anybody in the Argentine revival. Their stories show us men and their wives who started out with small beginnings but who have been used in mighty ways by a God who provides grace, strength, and anointing to normal people.

Osvaldo and Alejandra Carníval

"Pastor, tell me a miracle testimony!" The young man had just tied up his dog outside the church door and was in a hurry to hear a good story of God at work before running the ten blocks home again. Little did his parents imagine that he had made a decision for Christ and instead of walking the dog early each morning, Osvaldo was actually running with his pet so he could spend a little time with the pastor and then hurry back home. From early on, Osvaldo had been very interested in God's power to work miracles, and God rewarded that clear and open faith with much miraculous fruit.

One day in the office at River Plate Bible Institute I received a call from a very irate mother of an incoming freshman. "We have plans for our son. He's going to be someone influential with a good position in life. How do you dare accept him in your Bible 'school'?" Rather flabbergasted, I suggested she call his pastor. "I've already talked to him for half an hour," was her reply. Finally I recommended, "Why don't you allow God to do what He wants to do in your son's life?" Her son received his training, graduated, and worked at planting a church, and today one of the women's leaders and most faithful members of the church is Osvaldo's own mother.

When he was a freshman at IBRP he obtained permission from the military government to hold street meetings in the very center of Buenos Aires. The Federal Capital has the widest multiple-lane avenue running through it. He was able to get permission to hold evangelistic meetings right at the most critical place on that avenue, the Obelisk Monument. At a time when very few were brave enough to do street evangelism, he was coordinating the youth of his church to preach and worship with him at the Obelisk Plaza every Saturday night. Many times crowds would reach one hundred fifty in attendance, with eight to nine lanes of traffic going by on each side! God was preparing him in courage for the next big step of faith.

When Osvaldo graduated from IBRP and before he married Alejandra Lagraba, a young lady from the city of Rosario whom he had met at the Bible school, he invited missionaries Ralph and Frances Hiatt to work with them in founding a church in the Federal Capital neighborhood of Parque Patricios.

Each evening they would set up one hundred fifty wooden chairs at a wide place on the sidewalk that happened to be the exit of the subway. It was right in the middle of a wide avenue of the Federal Capital with all the noise of horns blaring and buses' motors revving up. But the faithful evangelists sang, preached, and prayed for people each night. Along with the superb example of ministry Osvaldo had in his pastor, Jose Manuel Carlos, he also was privileged to watch the lives and hearts of the Hiatts. On many occasions late in the evening, when the chairs had been folded up and everyone was ready to leave, Ralph continued to pray with a homeless man or an alcoholic.

After five months of meetings six times a week on the sidewalk of Rivadavia Avenue, the congregation had a building. The funds had been procured to purchase and remodel a warehouse. It was a great sight as happy people marched from the street location where they had been meeting to their new church home, ten blocks away on Avenida Eva Perón.

The church was very well-located just two blocks away from a city park. Often in those first months, the leaders would hold campaigns in the park. One strong crusade of thirty days in Parque Chacabuco was held about one year after the initial crusade with four hundred decisions for Christ. On one occasion some young men of the neigh-borhood thought they would mock the evangelists by get-ting in the prayer line at the end of the service, just for fun. What a surprise they had when they ended up on their backs, knocked to the ground by the power of God! Many of those young people became some of the first church leaders.

During the eighties, the church grew to 1,100 members. Though evangelism continued unabated, the number of new church attendees didn't seem to go beyond two hundred people each year. This barely seemed to compensate for the loss of people who moved away or stopped coming, keeping the church about even.

Then some of the ladies of the church's intercession min-istry began to feel some very strong pains in the area of their wombs. Initially, they thought it was a natural phenomenon, but when it happened with various ones simultaneously, God showed them that in reality He was allowing them to feel the spiritual birth pangs that would lead to many spiritual babies being born into the congregation. Just as Isaiah 66:7–9 and Paul, in Galatians 4:19 say, a time of intense spiritual labor pains so often accompanies the growth of Christ's church.

Near that time, in the beginning of the nineties, a strange event occurred in the Carníval home. Alejandra had the aid of a part-time household helper who would come in to assist the family. One day the young lady was ironing two or three creases into a pair of pants, so Alejandra walked over to show her how to do it correctly, and the lady fell down! Then the pastor's young boys fell to the ground. Thinking the maid was demonized and that the boys were having a physical prob-lem, Osvaldo tried to help but also went down to the floor. He came to realize that the power of God was at work.

This was a new thing for the pastor and his family, and it spread to the entire congregation. Services began to last four or five hours at a time. The people were lost in God's presence, enjoying His outpouring. The center of life for the congregation became their church and what the Holy Spirit was doing among them. Worship was very sweet, and there was a touch of joy that gave one a sense of the playfulness of God.

Catedral de la Fe became a revival center to be visited by hundreds of pastors and leaders from many denominations during this move of God. Profound changes began taking place in these churches as well, especially in worship, lifestyle, openness, and dependence on the Holy Spirit.

Sherry and I took our children to one of those services. When Sherry saw entire sections of the congregation falling to the ground, she hurried to the balcony, thinking she didn't want to fall if it wasn't real and neither did she want to be the only person left standing out of an entire section. When the pastor asked those who were hungry for a touch from God to go forward to receive prayer, our fourteen-year-old son, Nathan, went to the front with me. Everyone who walked across the platform fell under the heavy weight of God's glory.

Osvaldo had trained the ushers to pick them up off the wooden platform almost immediately so others could receive prayer. But when Nathan fell prostrate, Pastor Carníval instructed the leaders to leave him alone, and he lay under God's power for a long time. What tenderness this man of God showed to our son who was at such an important age developmentally. The Lord really moved in his life that day, and Pastor Carníval had been so sensitive in the Spirit to facilitate it.

Though the congregation lived months of that euphoria, finalizing the services at one or two o'clock, they were led into different stages of maturity and growth. One of the most important times was in 1997 when a sense of uneasiness began in Osvaldo's heart while his church was running 1,300. He felt overwhelmed with the needs of the people and the responsibility of caring for them as pastor. Then God led him to transform the structure of his congregation to a cell-based church. He states, "Now I owe myself to my twelve leaders and am available for them at every critical moment of their lives. Each of them does the same for their twelve and so on." At present the church has about 2,300 cell leaders and has grown to twenty thousand in attendance.

The services last several hours now instead of the four they once did, but Pastor Osvaldo states that this is a different stage with the emphasis being on multiplication. Every weekend fifty or more people respond per service to altar calls for salvation. The church has three services on Saturday and three on Sunday, along with the ministry through 3,500 cell groups.

During this time of growth, God placed in Pastor Osvaldo's heart a vision to touch the city of Buenos Aires. Miraculously, an opportunity was afforded the church to have a program on open television. This lasted nine years and has made the church and its pastor very well known.

Pastor Osvaldo has also had a major impact on other denominations, pastors, and nations through the cell-based ministry conference that the church holds annually. He and his wife, Alejandra, have held three cell-based church conferences thus far which Latin American pastors and leaders from around Argentina and other countries in Latin America have attended. I recently visited a church that had run a hundred in attendance for years but has now quadrupled in number because of the process of risk-taking growth that began when their pastors attended this conference. The Ukranian-origin congregation purchased a factory and transformed it into a church with a capacity for seven hundred. The best part of this change is that they are seeing dozens of unbelievers come to Christ every month.

Pastor Carnival and Pastor Pedro Ibarra have headed up a prayer movement for the city of Buenos Aires that began in 2001 during the worst economic crisis Argentina has ever experienced. Looting at supermarkets was rampant as were road blockades and *cacerolazos*, citizens' demonstrations that included pounding on pots and pans for hours. The *corralito*, or the bank's "little corral," had blocked the withdrawal of people's savings to prevent capital flight. Anger and bitterness were rampant.

The big prayer meeting at the Plaza de Mayo which began as the dream of one of our IBRP students took place in the midst of this dark time. That was the beginning of the pastors meeting together for prayer. The first few months, eight hundred pastors gathered to pray for two hours every Thursday morning. Though attendance at the prayer meeting is now one hundred pastors, they have prayed together faithfully every week for two-and-a-half years.

Pastor Carnival has sensed the Lord saying that the key to the nation is reaching the city, and the key to reaching the city is that each pastor and his congregation touch society with God's power. He believes this is the stage to penetrate every sector of society.

During the latest congressional and senatorial elections, Carnival invited various candidates to the church, allowed them to share, and also prayed for each of them without showing a preference. One of those candidates was soon put in charge of the federal prisons. When the need arose to have a pastor oversee the evangelical chaplaincy program for the Capital, the man in authority remembered the pastor who had ministered to his life and invited Carnival to fill that vital role.

In a recent critical situation involving provincial leadership, the government official assigned to handle the situation called Pastor Carnival for prayer. This led to several unique opportunities for ministry.

Pastor Osvaldo was recently chosen as one of two anchors for the Latin American version of *The 700 Club*. Not a man to push himself forward, he has dedicated himself to ministering to his own congregation, and God is opening doors for him to be a blessing beyond Argentina.

Osvaldo talked about his wife and how they have both developed together. He made an interesting observation that the Spanish word for *develop* is *desarrollar* which also means to unfold. He said a good marriage is like this. We unfold or unfurl each other, finding out what is inside the other. There are always surprises, fresh things to discover, and new joys to unwrap.

A man of great wisdom and tenderness, accompanied by a woman of stature in God, they make a great team for the expansion of the Lord's kingdom. Who could have imagined that the young man who responded to Ralph Hiatt's challenge to accept Christ there in the La Boca plaza would be ministering to thousands? Who could foretell that the youth who ran into the church asking his pastor for a fresh miracle story would himself be used to touch so many lives? God knew, and His purpose is being fulfilled. "Who hath known the mind of the Lord?" (Rom. 11:34).

GUILLERMO AND GRACIELA PREIN

What an experience it is to show up at Centro Cristiano Nueva Vida and observe the tremendous, vibrant life. The church runs over twenty-six thousand. Each week 1,135 prayer and miracle evangelistic cell groups function all over the city of Buenos Aires and another 549 pastoral or leadership cell groups meet at the church. The congregation holds forty different services on several campuses with the idea of providing a diverse series of days and times to meet the needs of different segments of society. The leadership also runs a twenty-four-hour radio station. "It is not so much to teach, as it is to accompany the believers," says Prein. "The radio station keeps people in the fire of the Holy Spirit all day long at work, and it communicates the culture and way of life of the church to those who do not belong to it."

Where did all of this begin? How did so much life get packed into one congregation?

Guillermo was one of seven key young men won to

Christ in the Boca neighborhood by Ralph Hiatt and Jose Manuel Carlos. They were all discipled by their pastor each day, beginning with prayer at seven o'clock. A critical part of their background had to do with Ralph Hiatt's mentoring. He was a great example of faith and had a tremendous passion for evangelism.

Another crucial aspect of this training had to do with their years of preparation at River Plate Bible Institute, where Guillermo met his wife, Graciela. Before they graduated, they were already pastoring in a slum-area church. This young pastor told his congregation to reach out to the lost, and suddenly the church was filled with prostitutes. "The normal make-up of that first congregation in Villa Tranquila, Avellaneda was one of prostitutes, drug addicts, and delinquents," Pastor Guillermo recalls.

Then Guillermo and Graciela invited missionaries Ralph and Frances Hiatt to be part of a church plant in the Federal Capital, a cooperative effort with the Boca Church pastured by Jose Manuel Carlos. The neighborhood chosen was the staunchly religious neighborhood of Parque Patricios. A large factory building was purchased and meetings were held in cooperation for a while, but the time came when the young couple was left to face the situation alone.

Tenacious in his faith, Guillermo began to preach twelve times per day on the street and one time at the church. The atmosphere was not very open or welcoming, leaving the young preacher with a black eye once in a while. A large building had been purchased and sat empty. By his own account, after preaching for six solid months, thirteen times a day, not one person was converted. That adds up to 6,379 street meetings and church services without a convert. "If I said the name of Jesus, people would turn around and leave," he says of that difficult time period.

Guillermo was despondent and thought seriously of giving up. It was then that God spoke to him and asked him how many people he could fit into the building. As he walked around and dreamt, he tried to consider where two or three hundred more could sit on balconies. He suddenly realized that he was thinking too small and that the Lord could give them thousands of converts. But then God spoke clearly to him and said, "Not thousands, but millions."

Twenty years later with a church of thousands of leaders trained and twenty-six thousand in attendance, it is much easier to imagine that possibility. The congregation meets on three campuses, including a five star hotel and a theater purchased in the heart of the city, and the church's influence is touching numerous neighborhoods and communities.

What happened to transform zero results into baptismal services in which more than nine hundred are baptized in water—three at a time? Part of the key has been the monthly miracle services, with amazing works of God in evidence. The church has a strong emphasis both on prayer and on believing God for miracles. Guillermo is convinced that the Lord used miracles to open people's hearts to teaching and preaching. From the time he graduated from IBRP, his ministry has been accompanied by miracles and deliverance from demonic possession.

Another aspect has been the miracle and prayer cell groups. Early on, Pastor Guillermo had realized the potential of the cell-based concept. However, growth was stymied until the Lord led him to hold evangelistic and prayer cell groups in homes or businesses and then to concentrate all of the leadership training and discipleship at the church. These leaders care for and pastor the people. "Our congregation is not a church of one pastor but of a body of pastors," according to Pastor Prein.

God is continuing to lead Pastor Prein into fresh perspectives regarding the cell groups and structures. The novel ideas aren't coming from leadership think tanks. Rather fresh ideas are given from the Holy Spirit in up to forty-two days of fasting and prayer by a pastor who seeks God for the answers.

Another key to sustained growth has been a love for people and a desire to meet their needs. Often Guillermo will say, "The pastor (same word as *shepherd* in Spanish) should have the smell of sheep on him." He believes that we have to be concerned about adding to the fold, and then we have to take care of the lambs. In a recent message at a national Assemblies of God pastors' conference Prein said, "What do we have? Passion for souls or passion for success? The problem is when the face of the individual is transformed into a number. When one has passion for souls, he quits thinking about how many there are and starts considering how the ones that we have are doing."

Guillermo and Graciela married after graduating from IBRP and have ministered in tandem very effectively. She is a behind-the-scenes person, very gifted in administration. How often the visionary people-oriented person needs at his side someone who will help give consistency and follow-through to the vision.

Sherry and I attended an International Banquet that the church held recently. This is not one of those events held in a basement fellowship hall. The pastors took a concept they learned in their time of training at IBRP and have transformed it into one more opportunity to evangelize effectively. Renting one of the largest convention centers in the city, they combined classy booths, traditional dress from each nation, and international foods with an evangelistic campaign each evening. Thousands attended and were touched by the Word and received a vision for the world.

The congregation has also reached out to hundreds of other congregations with practical backing and with evangelistic teams. Youth teams have gone into other countries, for example, and ministered very effectively, sometimes winning as many people to Christ through street evangelism as would happen in a large crusade.

The congregation is known for its faith for miracles and for its creativity in reaching out to the lost. July is the month of winter vacation when thousands of children are off school and parents line up for hours at children's theaters to help fill these days with family activities. Each year the church presents a professional drama for children, which is advertised around the city throughout the winter vacation, adding up to thirty-eight presentations during the two weeks the kids are off school. This is an opportunity for thousands of children and their families to be influenced by the principles of the Word. This year, more than forty-six thousand saw the drama, and 4,066 accepted Christ.

One of the daily papers in Buenos Aires has six daily editions with a circulation of almost two million. In order to whet the appetite of potential clientele, that paper was producing a "pocket newspaper," a version distributed free that was full-color and the length of a newspaper in size, but only three inches wide. Even before the secular newspaper, Centro Cristiano Nueva Vida began to produce *Red Vida*, a free, full-color, evangelistic newspaper, in that special format. It was filled with testimonies of healings and transformation and had a circulation of two hundred thousand.

It is Friday night at eight o'clock What would you expect to see if you visited Prein's church? Walk into the building that is next door to the main sanctuary and see the workers with the children, five hundred of them at least, worshiping the Lord. Then meander around the block to the youth area. Several of the youth cell groups are meeting out on the sidewalk. There is literally no room inside. To enter the youth area, one has to go through the intercessory prayer group, which is packed into the foyer. They seem totally immune to distraction. Inside about one hundred youth cell groups are piled practically on top of each other in the rented auditorium; the youth huddled together with their Bibles.

Then enter the main sanctuary and join in the eight thirty leadership service. It follows another service that started at six o'clock, followed by adult cell groups. Be sure to hang out after the two-and-a-half hour leadership service because sometime after midnight there will be hundreds of people moving into discipleship and leadership cell groups even at that late hour. The pastor still takes the time to meet with a visiting group from the U. S. The evangelist on staff says that their monthly water baptism service will be held that coming Sunday with five hundred new believers to be baptized. So much life is in evidence. God is at work!

CLAUDIO AND BETTY FREIDZON

"Mother, I need money to go dancing," young Claudio had asked. His mother, Beatriz (Beba), was a new convert, but God was giving her wisdom.

"Come by the church and get it," she offered. She was attending a church in Coghlan, the federal capital where my mother, Betty Jane, was adult Sunday school teacher. Beba's work as a cosmetic beautician put her in contact with many well-known actors and politicians. Often she would weep during a service and end up having to remove her false eyelashes. My mother took a personal interest in her and spent time disciplining her. Today Beba is a prayer warrior.

When young Claudio went by the church to get his partying money from his mother, he found the young people playing ping-pong and having a good time together. Though he received some stares of curiosity at first, there was a peace in the place that drew him in.

Soon he had surrendered his life to Christ and was participating in the youth group. Once while attending a youth retreat, Claudio heard God's voice calling him into the ministry. He and his wife, Betty, attended IBRP, graduated, and were about to join a communal-type church with strong authoritarian leadership when missionary Ralph Hiatt spoke to the pastor and said, "Not Claudio. I won't let you take Claudio." Looking back, this was a critical moment in the life of such tender, malleable ministers. A strong leader could have made them a part of his personal kingdom and affected their potential for life. Thank God for the wisdom and courage that Ralph Hiatt had to intercede forcefully on their behalf.

Though missionary Paul Brannan had already left the country for another assignment (Ralph Hiatt invited him back to help with this crusade), he trusted the young couple, who were engaged to be married and freshly graduated from Bible school. A small lot with a house on it was purchased in Parque Chas of the Federal Capital. Claudio and Betty would fold up the bed and put out the chairs for the small congregation. Their home was the church, so when services were held, they squeezed together their few belongings. One day a visiting pastor threw out a comment that challenged the young couple's faith. He looked around at the cramped quarters that doubled as church and one-bedroom apartment and said, "God cannot work here. It is too small!"

Claudio and Betty hit bottom. They had done their best, but it didn't seem like it was good enough. The sacrifice of their privacy, attempting to grow the church in their home—the only place they had available—apparently was deemed insufficient. On top of this, all their efforts to evangelize seemed to backfire. Five elderly ladies attended the church, and that was it. If Buenos Aires hit a spell of low temperature weather, the whole congregation, all five of them, would catch colds and be gone at the same time. There were services that Claudio preached to a congregation of one, his wife, Betty.

It was then that Claudio determined that he was not cut out to be a minister. "Betty," he said, "I'm going to hand in my credentials." A lump formed in Betty's throat as she watched her young husband walk toward the bus stop to go to his interview with the superintendent. Claudio had been so full of dreams, ideas, and creativity, and now his strength and determination seemed depleted by the hardness of reality.

When he was allowed in to see the national church leader,

he clutched his credentials in his hand and began to clear his throat. "Claudio, before you start, I just wanted to tell you that God has been speaking to me about you. I have had a strong impression that He is going to use you tremendously. Your ministry is going to have amazing fruit." This was the superintendent of Argentina talking about him! "Now, what was it that you wanted to talk about?"

"Just came to greet you," the young preacher muttered, half embarrassed and yet amazed at what he had heard his leader saying. Needless to say, he never turned in those credentials.

Still, difficulties persisted. One afternoon he was very discouraged. "I wanted to avoid meeting up with others who might ask me how I was," Claudio recalls, "because I had no testimony at that moment. No strategy, no growth, no youth group. But God was dealing with us. He always has plans."

Soon Betty's uncle, Nicanor, came to visit them and ministered at the church. In the middle of the service—which no one had attended—he said, "The Lord has a word for you, brother. He shows me something clearly. God is showing me multitudes. I see your church, and it is thousands and thousands of people who are lining up to get in. Now I see you going out of the country, and I see stadiums full of people in Latin America and all over the world."

"And I had an empty church," Claudio recalls. One evening after the few people had left, Uncle Nicanor asked him, "Claudio, what do you see?"

"I closed my eyes, and I saw nothing at all," Claudio states. "All I could see was empty chairs."

After praying in tongues for a while Betty's uncle declared, "God is going to change your ministry, and your ministry will impact many."

Claudio closed his eyes again and repeated, "I don't see anything."

God's envoy ended with a quiet challenge, "You keep calm, brother, because even though you do not see it, believe it."

So Claudio said, "OK, I believe it."

The next Sunday the five or six little grandmothers between eighty and ninety years old were back, and Claudio stated to them, "God has spoken to me, and we are going to grow to fifty thousand in this church."

Claudio laughs as he recalls this. "Their false teeth about fell out when they heard that." God was beginning to stir his spirit through the prophetic ministry of others, but reality still seemed far removed from what was being said to him.

The church began to grow slowly and reached a hundred and thirty in attendance. Despite his young age, Claudio was elected presbyter of the Federal Capital section. During that time we asked him to teach theology at IBRP. He noticed several days running that his students looked extremely tired. "What's the matter? What have you been doing that you are so tired and fall asleep in my classes?" he asked.

"It is because we have been working at the campaign in La Plata where Carlos Annacondia is the evangelist," they explained. "We're seeing God do tremendous miracles." It was an hour and a half each way on the dilapidated Bible school bus. Most of the time, the students were getting back to the college at two or three o'clock in the morning, Claudio learned. No wonder they were falling asleep in class.

The teacher thought, "I should go check this out."

The evening he arrived at the campaign he was asked to go immediately to the intensive care tent to help with deliverance. "She's assigned to you," someone on the evangelist's team said, pointing to the form of a woman writhing on the ground. Dozens of people were in similar situations, being counseled and prayed for by pastors and by many of the IBRP students.

Leaning over the lady, the theology professor said, "Do you feel all right?" The distressed woman reached up and grabbed his tie and began to pull him every which way.

The knot on his tie ended up the size of a quarter as he was being choked and yanked around. Some of the team members came over and rescued him as he thought to himself, "I need to find out what my students have learned working here every night."

It was in those beginning years that Carlos Annacondia began to pray with two or three young pastors: Claudio Freidzon, Osvaldo Carnível and at times with Guillermo Prein. Claudio and Osvaldo taught the evangelist about theology and homiletics. Carlos taught them how to get a hold of God.

During that time Claudio had a dream about preaching the gospel in a plaza, Plaza Noruega, at the center of Belgrano, an upscale section of Buenos Aires. He thought the dream was far-fetched, but he shared it with Betty, and she thought it was ridiculous. He shared it with the church leaders, and they thought the same. But he could not get away from it. So in obedience, he procured a string of lights to put up, a wooden platform, and a public address system, and he contacted an evangelist to come preach the campaign. At the last moment, the evangelist cancelled, so he thought, "What do we do? Who is going to preach?"

The Holy Spirit answered, "You are going to preach."

"But I'm not an evangelist. I'm a pastor and teacher," Claudio reasoned. Still he could not get away from the persistent thought that he should be the one to preach. The small church began the campaign, which lasted three weeks. During those twenty-one days 1,300 people accepted Christ. That is ten times the size of the congregation that sponsored the campaign!

Many miracles occurred during this time. People listening from the high-rise apartments near the plaza were healed of back problems. A taxi driver who was contemplating suicide had parked his car near by and began listening to the Word. When he went forward and accepted Christ he "felt an indescribable peace" and that he was no longer the same desperate man. Well-dressed ladies in their fur coats walked over to see what was happening and then were knocked into the bushes by the power of God. Healings abounded, and so many lives were changed.

The young pastor did not realize, however, that as the staging ground for the campaign, he had unwittingly chosen the center of operations for a drug ring headed up by "*El Francés*," the Frenchman. God touched that young man's life during the campaign, freed him from addiction, and transformed him totally. Sergio the Frenchman became one of Claudio's key pastors, dedicated along with his family to serving God.

A large warehouse three blocks away was rented so the church could meet together. The dream was coming true. Soon Claudio was on the radio every night at midnight, and the congregation was growing constantly.

It was then that Claudio would go into the church office, not due to any personal problems, but because of his hunger for God. He and Pastor Pedro would always converse about the same topics; prayer, fasting, and revival. Those times of sharing brought faith and hope. Feeling challenged to expect more, Claudio would say, "There has to be more." On one of those occasions, Pastor Pedro Ebana said, "I have the answer for you," and handed him a copy of the book, *Good Morning Holy Spirit* by Benny Hinn. Claudio read it with hunger to know the Holy Spirit better, having grown dissatisfied with merely attending to the business of pastoring a large congregation.

"I must get to know the author of this book," he thought. So he and Betty invested most of their savings and bought a ticket to Miami. They attended the crusade that was going on, but initially were rebuffed by those in charge of crowd control. Chagrined, he thought, "All that sacrifice to get here, and I can't even have a five-minute talk with him."

That evening in the crusade service, evangelist Benny Hinn asked, "Do we have any visitors here from other countries?"

"Argentina!" Claudio yelled among the cacophony of other countries being called out.

"Come up to the platform, Argentina," Brother Hinn said. Amazed at this turn of events, Claudio walked up on the platform. The Lord's power knocked him to the floor, and it was then that another man of God gave him a prophesy. "You will travel to Sweden, Germany, all over Europe. You will be used of God in Africa...."

What a word from the Lord for a young pastor hungry for His presence. At the time it seemed almost unbelievable. The thought of reaching out to the three and a half million people of the federal capital area within an hour's drive of his church seemed enough of a challenge, but here was the Holy Spirit saying he would affect the nations of the world.

After Claudio and Betty had returned from that trip, he was sharing with his congregation what had happened, when he noticed that a couple of people in the back row had fallen down. Trying to gesture to the ushers to attend to those people, he waved his hand at them—and fifty people fell down! God began to work amazing miracles, and soon there were crowds of people waiting in line. The church had refurbished and moved into a skating rink because of the large crowds, but even this didn't seem to be enough. Pastors from all over Argentina traveled to be in the meetings.

José Manuel Carlos, our superintendent for the Assemblies of God for Argentina, told of visiting the church at this time and trying to get into the building. The line was very long around the church so he tried to slip in at the door. People who didn't recognize him said, "Hey, get in line. Who do you think you are?" but one of the ushers figured it out and let him in, taking him to the front of the church. "My knees were shaking together, and I felt so weak that I thought I was going to fall down before I even got in the church," says José Manuel. "I thought, what is this?"

"After the message, Claudio came down off the platform and started to minister," continues José Manuel. "As he came up to me, I fell down. Only I did it face first, and right on top of

Claudio. It happened so fast that neither of us were prepared, and I came to with my face in Claudio's face and with someone from Claudio's congregation yelling with urgency, 'He fell on the pastor! Get him off the pastor! Get him off the pastor!'"

IBRP students were among the first to attend the meetings in Belgrano. Some of them returned to their churches and without a word being spoken, the same signs began to be seen in other cities. Freshman students walked down the aisle of their church, and people would fall out in the power of the Holy Spirit on both sides of the aisle.

I remember when Claudio would call the pastors up to the front, fifty of them at a time. When he prayed, they all went down in a heap. The same happened to the pastors' wives. This had to be God. Argentines are very careful about their dress, and to see these leaders all piled on top of each other was truly amazing. I have watched presbyters who no one touched being thrown backwards by the power of God. They ended up on their backs, kicking feverishly, lost in the power of the Spirit. Other leaders have fallen in the Spirit up to twenty times in a single night as God dealt with their lives, and some of the starchiness was knocked out of them.

Some key pastors from Berlin gave a testimony when they visited IBRP. "There is a before and an after with the history of the church in Berlin," they said. "Before Claudio Freidzon came to minister and afterwards." There are many other cities and nations that could give the same testimony.

Within a few weeks, God was leading Claudio to rent a small stadium to handle the crowds and then the Velez Sarsfield stadium with a capacity of sixty thousand for Easter Sunday. Even this huge stadium was filled to the glory of God.

Claudio has traveled to more than fifty nations in these ten years and has been powerfully used by the Lord to revive the church in so many places and to inspire thousands to believe. He has been the speaker for conferences and evangelistic campaigns in situations as diverse as a pastor's conference in

Burkina Faso and a Holy Spirit conference in Australia. Pastor Freidzon has spoken face-to-face (not including the media) to over three million people and is well-loved by the Christian leadership of nations around Latin America and the world.

Betty and Claudio travel to some corner of the earth almost every week but are back in their church to minister through the weekend. Betty is also a preacher and speaks at many of the conferences herself. Claudio has encouraged and supported Betty in her own ministry opportunities, and she often is one of the rotating preachers at the Breakthrough Conferences. Breakthroughs are held for pastors and other church leaders annually at the Rey de Reyes Church, but they are also taken into other settings internationally, including the United States.

The congregation is reaching out, not only to other nations through the ministry of their pastor, but also to different provinces of Argentina through a ministry called Operation Blessing. Claudio and a large team from his church work with the pastors of different cities where a stadium is rented and a crusade is held. This evangelistic outreach is run in conjunction with a compassion program that is designed to touch the lives of many poor people affected by the economic crisis. Up to thirty thousand people at a time have attended and hundreds have made decisions for Christ through these events. The fruit is being carefully followed up through cell-based church principles.

Rey de Reyes (King of Kings) Church now has twelve thousand members and a leadership base of 1,600. The choir and worship team have recorded CDs that have spanned the globe. Twenty years after the Plaza Noruega campaign, twelve years after the anointing began, there are still lines of people three or four blocks long waiting to get into one of the four services held each Sunday. The newly enlarged sanctuary will help for a while, but not permanently. The demonstrations of God's power have not diminished. Each service has two messages, a brief one first for the unbelievers after which there is an altar call. Most services thirty or forty people go forward to accept Christ, and the church keeps advancing. God's promises are coming true.

PEDRO AND GERTRUDIS IBARRA

Recently graduated from IBRP, Pedro and Gertrudis Ibarra took charge of a church building with no congregation. The church had not been used due to the discredit before the community for three years. Pedro and Gertrudis evangelized house to house and preached on the street corners, but hardly anyone showed up.

After three years of no results and feeling the anguish of failure, he resolved to seek God with fasting and prayer. His friend, José Manuel Carlos, would accompany him to encourage him in those difficult days. Something happened the third day of fasting. "It was surprising, like a spiritual breakthrough where God filled the place," states Ibarra. He sensed a supernatural authority and began to cry out "In the name of Jesus . . . in the name of Jesus." This went on for quite some time until "Spiritually, I saw the darkness disappear from the place and grotesque figures leave because they could not withstand the power of the name of Jesus. It seemed like heaven itself came to back up the name of Jesus."

Pastor Pedro realized that the victory was real. That same day at 6:00 p.m., the first person showed up at church and was saved and delivered of spiritual problems due to involvement with the occult. Pedro continued to seek God until he heard the promise, "For I give you the center of the city." He was obedient and began to preach in the central plaza of the city of Quilmes. A theater was rented and later purchased. Now a church building for five thousand has been erected and the congregation numbers in the thousands.

"God, all-powerful, stands behind those He calls. What human weakness. What divine success," Pedro exclaims.

Wrap-Up

The characteristic that stands out in each of these key personalities is faith. The Lord speaks to these pastors, and they act on it. That takes faith. Each of them guards his devotional and personal life from cynicism, sarcasm, and from the influence of people that contradict a life of risk-taking belief in the Holy Spirit's power.

How is faith produced? By the Word. It works by contact with people of faith—by an intense desire to be a person of faith. By the very need when there is no option but to step up and believe God to act. This lifestyle of faith has led these revival pastors to take their people into new realms, and the kingdom of God is clearly being advanced to His glory.

Exactly how does all this work? What are some of the lessons these pastors have learned as they seek to lead a move of God? They have indeed been in the school of revival.

5

Pastoring the Revival

ISTORICALLY THE AVERAGE duration of a widespread revival is just several years. Mortals wear down. Prosperity sets in because of the blessing of God and the upward lift of the gospel. People find they need time for the concerns of goods and everyday affairs. So all-night prayer vigils and late-night services are out of the question. Meeting at the church for prayer at five o'clock seems ludicrous. The revival turns into a bittersweet memory rather than something to be lived. It becomes impractical to continue.

Quite a number of Welsh immigrants live in southern Argentina. Hard economic times in their own land combined with the guidance of the Holy Spirit to send them to the sheep herding lands of Patagonia. Many of the people still tell stories that were passed down about the revival in Wales in 1904, and it wasn't so long ago that the old men used to get together and reminisce in melancholy tones about those amazing days. However, even this famous revival only lasted three years.

So why has this present move of God lasted for more than twenty years in Argentina? Some would say that it only exists in three or four well-known churches and that the revival has actually been over for a quite a while. But the pastors don't really see it that way. They know God is at work in their churches.

Alberto Romay, a graduate of our school who is now an evangelist and pastor, came to talk with me this week. He is raising funds for a small piece of land in a very poor area of the city of Rosario so they can build a church. His congregation is so poor that he has been traveling in revival services for four years. He loves the lost and definitely wants to encourage the church, but part of his motivation is that he needs to raise offerings for his own church building. What would be available from the banks in many countries has to be a matter of prayer and creativity in the slum areas of his city.

I asked him if the power of God was only evident in three or four areas of Argentina. "Not at all!" he responded adamantly. Then he started to name province after province and pastor after pastor across denominational lines where He has seen the Lord's power at work even in the last few months. He recounted numerous healings and other testimonies of God's power and grace.

Evangelist Romay has seen many miracles of God's power including healing for deaf-mutes, deafness, stuttering, thyroid tumor, breast cancer, broken bones, sterility, anorexia, bulimia, alcoholism, addiction to nicotine, and rheumatic fever.

Although there are dangerous attitudes that can destroy any revival, we feel very thankful to God that He is still pouring out His grace and power. He has raised up many leaders who have stayed steady throughout these waves of revival.

One of the main reasons that the refreshing throughout Argentina has not dissipated into strife or exhaustion is that most of the key personalities in this revival are not visitors or traveling speakers, but rather pastors. They desire the steady growth of their people and the continuing work of the Spirit in their churches. The Lord of the church has given these pastors insight and practical wisdom to know how to care for the flock in the midst of this amazing move.

Mi Buen Pastor

There is a beautiful Spanish chorus entitled "Jesús, Eres Mi Buen Pastor" (Jesus, You Are My Good Shepherd).[1] The word for *shepherd* here is exactly the same as that for *pastor*.

The pastors of this revival have a great concern for individuals. They have a heart for keeping track of people and seeing that everyone is growing and serving the Lord. Even in the large churches, they have developed ways of knowing where people are at in their walk with God.

Guillermo Prein told me a story once about a pastor of a smaller church in his town who called and asked about a particular church member of his who was apparently having problems with a church member of Prein's. He told him the story and Pastor Prein said he would get back to him on it. Within a matter of just several hours, even with his church membership of thousands, Prein was able to locate the leader of that person's group and find out exactly what was happening. He actually had more information than the other pastor who later asked, "How did you do that? You have thousands to consider, and you get the real story so quickly?"

It is because these pastors care about their flocks and have set up a system whereby people are nurtured and ministered to individually. There is a security with that kind of shepherd. Jesus comes after us, finds us and pulls us back out of danger. These caring pastors and their trained leaders are just like that.

The pastors here are not in a hurry. They love the altars. They pray for folks, lay hands on them, wait around in the presence of the Lord while God touches people. They observe and watch where God is moving and who has needs. They sometimes tramp back into the audience to find someone they have noticed and minister to them.

When they pray with groups and those people are touched, they don't just walk off. They watch that all are cared for and continue to facilitate the move of the Lord in these peoples' lives. Many times they go back to pray again for people, a second or even a third or a fourth time.

Even the busiest pastors care. I have seen many give up an afternoon off to minister to a visiting group and spend several hours longer than planned. When God is moving, they are not in a hurry. I have noted people taking deep sighs of peace and relief as they realize the pastor is still there, hovering around, caring. It helps to have an overseer and know everything is in order. There's a security to that, and it brings a smile. That's what Jesus would do, "Mi Buen, Pastor."

Perhaps it is also this pastoral core that brings them all to care so much for those who do not yet know Christ. There is such a passion for souls.

Vision and a Burden

How refreshing it is to be around the pastors here and to see that most of them have such a large vision. Dreams could involve buildings or notoriety or anything, but here they always seem to be tied in directly to winning the lost.

I remember well the moment, even before the strong move of God in his church, that Claudio Freidzon shared with our students on a day of fasting and prayer. He said that he and his wife were believing for fifty thousand souls. At the time, I thought he had lost his senses. Fortunately, I did not express this negative judgment to anyone. God has certainly proven me wrong.

It was in 1991 that missionary Steve Hill, Pastor Héctor Ferreyra, and I went out for ice cream. Together they had recently planted a church in Neuquén, southern Argentina. The church had grown to eleven hundred in a year. I remember that on the back of a placemat they wrote the names of the ten cities where they desired to plant churches. Though God is using Steve and Jeri in other areas of the world, they continue to be close to Héctor and that original vision for Argentina is still strong.

Pastor Héctor feels that the Lord has given him the number of twenty thousand new converts, and he says that they are progressing consistently toward that goal. Two strong central churches and thirty-four other congregations have all been planted since 1990. They have three hundred cell groups and have been renting or purchasing movie theaters to plant churches in little towns within a one hundred kilometer radius of Neuquén.

Pastor Osvaldo Carníval has a heart to impact the city of Buenos Aires. He watched in frustration as they won so many new people but always tended to stay at 1,300 members, that is until 1997. God moved powerfully through the burden of the intercessors in their congregation, especially some women who actually felt the birth pangs as they tarried in prayer for the lost. The Lord showed Pastor Carnival how to coordinate a cellular church, and now they carefully disciple and pastor the new people. Their growth in the last seven years has multiplied to twenty thousand believers. Most leaders would have been thrilled with the 1,300, but Pastor Carnival desires to see thousands come into the kingdom of God and is concerned for each one's growth and incorporation into the church body.

Pastor Guillermo Prein has reached out to help one hundred different congregations in various countries during the last eight years. His own church is ministering to more than twenty-six thousand people in two different locations with forty services per week between them. The church holds eight major events a year, four baptisms and four other special services that bring together over ten thousand people each. The desire is to build the kingdom of God, not a personal kingdom. Love for those who do not know Christ is behind all of the effort, vision, and faith. The quarterly baptismal services of Centro Cristiano Nueva Vida run one hundred fifty people minimum and upwards to nine hundred.

New Life Christian Center has about 549 pastoral cell groups and 1,135 evangelistic prayer and miracle cell groups. They have a medical doctor, Dr. Aníbal Vassalli, who is in charge of documenting the healings. During the year 2000 they registered over one thousand miracles, including two resurrections. In 2004 they documented 1,558 miracles. People come to know Christ when they see how great God is.[2]

Both Guillermo Prein and Osvaldo Carníval had the same two mentors: their pastor José Manuel Carlos, a man of tremendous vision for new works, and also missionary Ralph Hiatt, a man of amazing passion for those who do not know Christ. Close ties are continued by the young pastors with those who have been mentored by such men.

Recently Pastor Carníval told me he had called Pastor José Manuel for his birthday. "It is a spiritual principle," he said. "The one who sows should reap. The time I spent being formed with him was very important." Pastor Carníval went on to speak of Ralph Hiatt, the man who won him to the Lord. "He showed me surrender with no limits, a passion for souls, and a willingness to give all and not expect anything. These things have marked me a great deal. A person influences 20 percent by what one says and 80 percent by what one is."

The pastors mentor new leaders and future pastors. They take time to care for the next generation and invest significantly in their lives. This kind of pastoring pays off!

LAY LEADERSHIP

The revival would have weakened a long time ago were it not for the mentality of participation fomented by the pastors who train up and give responsibility to numerous volunteer workers. These kingdom-builders are loyal to their pastors and make church their lives. They are willing to put their time and material goods at the disposition of the church.

In 1990, when Steve Hill spoke with Pastor Héctor Ferreyra about helping them to plant the church in southern Argentina, Héctor was already pastoring his own church in the city of Rosario. He had a growing congregation with three hundred members. But the Lord spoke to him about moving eight hundred miles south to wind-blown Neuquén to participate in opening that church. Twenty-five of his lay workers from Rosario pulled up roots and moved with him and his wife into the unknown. Each had prayed and felt God was leading them to go with their pastor. No wonder that church was running 1,100 in a year!

Becoming an *obrero* or worker is a major privilege in Pentecostal churches. As someone has said, "To be a pastor in Latin America you have to be a general because everyone in the church wants to be a sergeant, a corporal, or a captain."

Pastoring the revival has meant giving specific and careful attention to the nurturing of leaders. Their spiritual health and commitment are critical to fulfilling God's vision. It is amazing to hear how many faith workers each congregation has. For a larger church the number of lay leaders numbers in the hundreds.

Pastor Carnival talks about the necessity of awakening the leadership. He notes that in a traditional church the pastor does everything; he is like the director of an orchestra. "We changed to teams," he said, "and now we have moved the limits back even further. Now we have a church of leaders." This is certainly the case because there are about 2,700 leaders in that congregation alone. They do much equipping and training.

Everybody has twelve people they oversee. "It is easy to let a church become an orphanage with no father. A director is simply running back and forth, resolving problems, but not caring for people. However, I want to have a church that is a family. There are no orphans in a family, and there is always a father." Carnival believes that when a church grows past three hundred, the pastor will automatically be conflicted, having tension about who should get his time. But in the cell approach, even the pastor has just twelve to worry about. "There is no question," Carnival says. "Those are the people you pour yourself into."

In Carníval's eyes, this means that the pastor needs to relinquish control. However, he should not relinquish leadership.

BOLD FAITH AND A SPIRIT OF AUTHORITY

The leadership giftings in Argentina evidence a beautiful spirit of authority. This seems to fall upon the pastors of the revival like a mantle. They just know they will have to take care of situations, and they are ready for it. The pastors have a God-given boldness to handle problems, any disturbances that might occur during the services, and other situations that may be awry. Pastors confront people who need correction. They are firm with their own workers as may be needed. The anointing of the Holy Spirit provides an evident stability.

If someone is out of order, they are taken out of the service. This immediate correction would not be possible without a team concept. There may be as many as 1,600 volunteer workers in for the church services, and they are trained and ready to help. There are a lot of services, so many workers are also necessary. In any given service there are dozens who have the authority to step up and maintain order. They work in this boldness.

It is comforting to see the strong men and women serving as ushers, guiding the people, ready to pray with anyone, and trained to handle emergencies. They sit on the front rows. Several stand on each side of the platform, and others sit on the side in chairs. Some stay in the back and out in the foyer. Everywhere there is a strong sense of leadership. This provides a feeling of security for everyone involved as situations are handled when necessary. The sense of strong faith and anticipation by these leaders is also apparent. They believe that God is going to work.

The pastors also have an authority in spiritual things. They need to cast out demons, so they have a team of lay people who are trained in "liberación" or deliverance. Many times a tent out in back of the church or even the church kitchen has doubled as "intensive care" centers where demons are expelled in the name of Jesus.

However, the pastors don't strut around like spiritual John Waynes. They simply accept the fact that authority is needed and that God has entrusted them with power to heal the sick and cast out demons. "The mantle of authority is worn in humility. It is a beautiful combination," according to Dr. Carolyn Tennant, a university professor who has interviewed key pastors as part of the three classes on revivals that she taught in Buenos Aires.

The pastors have faith that is wonderful to see. Not afraid to take giant steps, they make strong moves like rent major stadiums and theaters, purchase large warehouses for church buildings, and rent land and tents to hold big campaigns and advance the church. This boldness is contagious, and the people follow their leaders willingly. Because they have stepped out with their pastor, they have no qualms about evangelizing openly. The people have already contributed time and funds freely, so why not go all the way and share about Jesus? They get excited to be a part, catching that passion for souls from their pastor.

This faith also brings a willingness to move in the gifts of the Spirit. Leaders and laymen alike take that first bold step to lay hands on the sick or to cast out a demon. Why not believe? God will do it. They move in the prophetic and words of knowledge. They expect miracles.

This boldness extends to approaching governmental leaders and congressmen, even the president, for what is desired. They have an interest in these peoples' lives and also in advancing God's kingdom. Approvals have come that once seemed impossible. Doors have opened. God is at work.

Openness

In speaking with the various pastors of the revival, another aspect stands out. They have been very teachable by the Holy Spirit and have been willing to grow and change. They are flexible. Self-evaluation as well as church evaluation have been part of their lifestyles. A willingness to observe others and to apply the truths they have learned has helped them to stay fresh.

One illustration of this would be how Pastor Guillermo Prein defines leadership. He gives God credit for showing him that a leader is a man or woman who has learned to resolve his or her problems in God. Once the person's practical experience lines up with the Word in every area, he can help others resolve their problems through God. The leader is not handed a thick, three-ring binder full of answers to be passed on to his disciples. He just spends time with the new believers without an agenda or having a specific lesson to be taught. He becomes their friend, and as they converse, scriptural principles are applied.

Pastor Prein sensed the Lord telling him that they already had a great deal of the Word being taught in the different services and the night Bible school at their church. Therefore, this non-structured approach to discipleship came in the midst of prayer and application of truth to reality.

Every new believer is told that he or she is a potential leader. The 549 pastoral cell groups at New Life Christian Center meet as circles of friends who help each other with problems on their life journeys.

Isn't that exactly what we all long for: someone to listen and really care, a fellow-pilgrim who is a brother and a friend? It is the way Jesus grew new leaders!

Accountability

This friendship along the journey is also modeled by the pastors themselves. For example, from the beginning of Brother Carlos

Annacondia's campaigns, he and various pastors started meeting weekly for prayer. Men like Claudio Freidzon and Osvaldo Carníval were in the group. These young pastors taught Carlos Annacondia doctrine, how to interpret Scripture and how to preach. He taught them faith and how to pray with authority.

One of the beautiful by-products of these weekly prayer meetings has been a special unity among a group of pastors that God has used so mightily. They schedule several hours per week to pray together, to seek God's presence, and to share testimonies.

These constant check-ups with each other have served to keep their walk pure and have prevented the revival from being snarled up and immobilized because of some moral lapse or because of arrogance. The deep friendship between these men has strengthened each of them individually and given consistency to their congregations and to the revival as a whole. It is not at all unusual to see them come to meetings at the others' churches, arriving quietly and sitting in the congregation.

Cooperation

Though this move of God has been Pentecostal and charismatic in its worship, expectation and practice, thankfully, to this point, it has not resulted in divisiveness. Congregational, Lutheran, Presbyterian, Anglican, Southern Baptist, and Assemblies of God fellowship leaders have sought God together, finding unity of heart and worship but not translating that unity to a necessary uniformity of practice or theological minutiae. As Carlos Mraida states in his paper "Unity as a Sign of Revival":

> "For several years now, the Holy Spirit has been producing a beautiful move of unity among pastors of all denominations here in Argentina. In each city, the fellowship among the Lord's servants of different denominations and ecclesiastical traditions has been growing. Ghosts of the past have faded away, mutual trust has

increased and the spirit of unity is pervasive. This growth in unity goes hand in hand with the remarkable growth of the gospel in Argentina. That is to say, unity has been a cause of revival and, at the same time, it is a product of revival."[3]

I have recently spoken with a congregational pastor whose church tripled in the last year because of the outpouring of God's power. Also, it was a joy to hear from a Slavic Pentecostal pastor that his congregation has grown from two hundred to more than eight hundred in the last two years since he and his leadership attended a cell-based church conference hosted by Pastor Osvaldo Carníval at Catedral de la Fe.

Even whole churches work together. Evangelist Carlos Annacondia's eight-month crusade in the city of La Plata would have had very little impact had it not united the congregations of the city and surrounding areas. Some eighty-three thousand people made decisions for Christ. Over forty congregations made it a priority to work with Brother Annacondia and his team.

When in the next months, he and his fledgling team took the message to the suburb of Buenos Aires called San Martín, over 142 congregations participated from denominations as diverse as the Assemblies of God, Christian and Missionary Alliance, Baptist, Open Bible, Nazarene, Mennonite, Foursquare, Pentecostal Holiness, and Lutheran congregations. That campaign produced fifty-seven thousand decisions for Christ. Most churches just cancelled services for an entire month, placing all their effort, manpower and time in cooperating with the campaign. One full month without regular tithes and offerings is true commitment. Then in Mar del Plata a few months later ninety-three thousand made decisions for Christ. Once again, scores of congregations made it a priority to work with Brother Annacondia and his team.[4]

Argentine churches had extremely challenging budgets

to meet during those days, but they put aside their own agendas and sought God together. Of course there were many who did not cooperate, and most of those churches have not grown. But those that became a part of what the Lord was doing now have six hundred or more in attendance. The Holy Spirit did a fresh work in all the churches.

Initially in the strong move of God breaking out at King of Kings Church in Belgrano, there was some competition and seeming attempts to duplicate what was happening there. Soon, however, each church fit into its own groove and major events in one would receive the backing and cooperation of others. For example, when Claudio Freidzon made the enormous decision of faith to rent the Velez Sarsfield Stadium with a capacity for sixty thousand people on Easter Sunday, 1993, hundreds of pastors cancelled services to participate in the event. The stadium was filled to capacity, to the glory and honor of the Lord Jesus and His church, not one local church. A united front was evident to the society.[5]

When evangelist Dante Gebel announced that God had led him to hold a meeting of more than one hundred thousand young people who would gather in the capital city at the Ninth of July (Independence Day) Obelisk, once again hundreds of pastors responded, encouraging the participation of their youth in an event that captured the imagination of the city and the church around the nation. They determined to declare together their allegiance to Christ and commitment to moral purity. More than six hundred long distance buses came from the provinces for that special day of celebration and covenant.

Dante has taken his praise and commitment gatherings to the provinces throughout the last years and has had stadiums filled with up to fifteen thousand young people at a time declaring God's glory.

Shortly after the large youth event at the Obelisk, some two hundred fifty thousand evangelicals paraded through the streets of Buenos Aires, singing songs of praise to the

Lord and also asking for legal recognition from the government as churches and not merely as social associations.

HARD WORK

These kinds of events take a lot of effort on everybody's part; otherwise they would never occur. After so many years, a sacrificial spirit is still evident in the pastors of the revival. It takes intense, sold-out, hard work to pastor a revival. That is the title of one of the paragraphs of our newsletters to supporting churches and friends.

The article states, "So many memories of the surprising schedules we have to keep come to our minds—pastors who night after night hold services and then pray for the sick and needy until after midnight. The normal time for eating supper for many of them has become one thirty or two o'clock in the morning. A few days ago I called a pastor, and his wife mentioned that he wasn't in. As I commented on how busy he must be, she said, 'Yes, we hardly have any time together. But it is worth it for the fruit of these days. We have to take advantage of them!'"

The newsletter continues, "God's Spirit has thrust evangelists, pastors, and lay workers into the most amazing situations. They have started open-air campaigns in the dead of winter and broken ground on building projects with no money at all to work with and no way to borrow money. Scores of us found ourselves in the thick of spiritual warfare, praying for healing and deliverance in situations we wouldn't have dreamed possible before. It has become a natural part of church life here to believe God to heal hernias, varicose veins, and kidney disorders. So many churches have found themselves time after time dealing with things they would once have thought impossible. But God!"

In the days when Carlos Annacondia held his first evangelistic campaigns in La Plata, some of the leaders did not even bother to undress when they went to bed. Someone was always coming in the middle of the night, asking for healing or bringing a person who was demon-possessed, and they had to be ready to help. That takes commitment.

Staying Put

Staying put also takes commitment. Pastoring in Argentina is a "till death do us part" proposition. People assume that the shepherd God gave them is for life. His personality and ministry are intertwined with them for good.

That is the mentality concerning church government here. In the Assemblies of God, by the constitution, it takes a two-thirds majority just to hold a vote of confidence, and even then it is merely a suggestion, with the pastor having the final say.

This can at times be insidious, especially if the leadership begins to lord it over the flock and act like they own it. But the fact that by and large churches never vote out their pastors means that both pastors and their flocks live in stability and avoid consuming energy on subterfuge or in-house politics. It has also meant that the focus can be on worship, winning the lost, growth, and discipleship. Yes, there are personality differences, and we do have situations where there is a falling-out between people, but most of the time the damage is controlled by that ingrained stability.

Linked to a Church

This connectedness helps in other ways as well. For example, although Claudio Freidzon travels to some country of the world almost every week, he rarely is gone from his own congregation on the weekend. He travels Monday evening and is back by Thursday to spend Friday through Sunday with his own people and his family. Although it has been a grinding schedule, it has given him a base of stability; an identity.

The church has participated in reaching out to five continents and more than fifty countries of the world through their pastor's ministry. More than three million people have been involved in a campaign with their pastor, and this is face-to-face ministry, not including the extensive television and video ministry.

However, besides encouraging their pastor in these outreaches, the people and leaders have participated in providing a church home, an electric place of worship and commitment where he is accepted, honored, and loved. His emotional tank is replenished at King of Kings Church. His close friends are among his staff and other ministers in Buenos Aires. Claudio cannot forget who he is because he is surrounded by people who care and believe in what God is doing through his life.

This same pattern holds true for various other ministers who are so used of God in Europe or other countries of Latin America, spreading the fire of revival and commitment. They always do it out of a solid local church base.

Involvement of the Pastor's Wives

It should be obvious by now that pastoring the revival here has not been the individual, disconnected, misunderstood ministry of a lone ranger with a personal vision. Rather it has been a team effort, and another major aspect of this is the pastor's family.

The pastors' wives have been totally involved in ministry at their husbands' sides. Without assuming a formal position, they have been seen as shepherdesses (*pastoras*) in the minds and hearts of their people.

How refreshing it has been to see Betty Freidzon at her husband's side, leading worship, teaching, and prophesying at their own church as well as on the platforms of countless conventions and stadiums around the world. Alejandra Carníval has been a key player in the long-term revival at Catedral de la Fe Church. Gertrudis Ibarra is a committed warrior at her husband's side in Quilmes. Graciela Olier in Mar del Plata fills a critical role in that impacting congregation. Isabel Scataglini is at the side of her husband, Pastor Alberto Scataglini, in La Plata, and there's the great ministry team of Sergio Scataglini and his wife, Kathy. Graciela Prein is a strong woman leader working with Guillermo. I could certainly go on, and the list would be a long one, especially considering the fact that there are some great women pastors as well.

What is interesting is that the ministry is at the center of these pastors' lives and their wives are integrally involved. They have a shared passion for the lost and for preserving new believers through discipleship. There is too much pressure on those in ministry to be able to withstand the onslaught alone. Husband and wife tandem teams have been very effective.

Usually the wives sit on the platforms or on the front row with their husbands. From this vantage point they can model the closeness of their relationship to other people and keep some precarious and sticky situations from occurring.

The Children, Too

In so many cases the pastors' children are also very much involved in the revival. They practically live at the church and are involved in the praise teams, all-night prayer vigils, cell groups, and various services each week. Ultimately the life of the entire family is concentrated in their church and in God's vision.

Perhaps one of the best signs is that 25 percent of the resident student enrollment at River Plate Bible Institute is composed of pastors' kids. These "PKs" want to follow their parents into the ministry. It is encouraging to see that they are not disillusioned and running from God. These young people are leaders in their own right.

I remember a typical night when the youth at King of Kings Church had one of their monthly all-night Friday to Saturday morning prayer vigils. Daniela Freidzon, Claudio, and Betty's daughter, led the worship and prayer time, and God's power was manifested in a special way. For the Saturday night service Daniela happened to be leading worship just before Pastor Claudio was to speak. As he was about to take the microphone from her she turned toward him, and he was knocked to the floor by the power of God. He could not get up for the duration of the service, which was spent in deep worship and praise. God's anointing is on the next generation also!

An Innovative Spirit

The young people bring freshness, which is another important aspect of pastoring this revival. Leadership has been willing to try various approaches and new church structures as well as allow fresh emphases and contemporary styles of music. The pastors have been open to learn, to change, and to receive. This has been crucial.

I remember a service recently in a Pentecostal church in Morón along with a youth evangelism team from Florida. The church began the service by stacking up all the chairs and piling their coats on the platform. Then they started to praise the Lord with so much freedom that we ended up doing a Jericho-type march, but it was more a train of singers, running out the doors of the church and all the way around the block. Perhaps we looked a little different but the neighborhood sure became aware that the church existed and that we have an exuberant faith.

As I looked at those coats heaped up that night, I thought what a contrast it was to the time some very religious people piled their coats at the feet of a young zealot called Saul of Tarsus. They were willing to kill in order to maintain control of their religious system. That same zealot would state with firm conviction a few years later: "Where the Spirit of the Lord is, there is liberty" (2 Cor. 3:17). *Teach us not to worship our systems, Lord.*

The churches are constantly coming up with ideas about reaching people. Pastor Prein's downtown campus is a theater right in the Buenos Aires theater district. Recently their arts group called *Artenenes* put on a play from the middle of July through the first part of August. This is the winter vacation time for the school children here in Argentina, and families traditionally do many things with their children during this time. The play drew in many children and adults and was an excellent example of good children's theater. With bright, contemporary costumes coupled with humor, music, and choreography, the drama troupe told the story of Ruth and Boaz. At the end a clear gospel message was presented, and young people were prepared to do follow-up among the attendees. Their total audience during winter vacation was more than twenty-five thousand. They put on thirty-eight different presentations and were rejoicing in the 4,066 decisions for Christ. What a creative witness!

Other outlets for the arts are a part of what God is doing in revival. Music takes on new beats and sounds, as well as prophetic songs. Once again, Pastor Prein's church is reaching out in creative ways to groups that they call "urban tribes" (young people involved in dark and gothic subcultures). The youth ministry to this generation is called *Urbanizarte*. In some neighborhoods they reach out with traditional *cumbia* music. Recently their concert called "Rock/Vida (Rock/Life)" drew eighteen thousand young people. The Holy Spirit is always creative.

The pastors are open to fresh ways that God wants to work, but they are not into fads, nor do they allow anything that is unscriptural. They are discerning and wise.

Building on Truth

Pastors of the revival have been very aware that they are stewards of God's truth and must render an accounting of the lives under their care. They have not run after new teachings, but rather there has been a searching of the Scriptures together to avoid heresy.

These pastors reject the tendency to live a disjointed Christianity that flits from fad to fad, from forgotten truth to forgotten truth, or from newfound truth to even newer truth. The pendulum swings between grace and the law, structured worship and total freedom in worship, the vertical relationship with God and horizontal relationships among men.

How refreshing it was to hear Pastor Carnível say that they do their utmost to build on each truth or principle they have been taught. They appreciate new insight, but they don't forget the earlier awareness of truth brought by the Paraclete.

Balance: Staying the Course

For years Sherry and I along with our children have attended Avance Cristiano, an Assemblies of God church pastored by our good friend, Edgardo Muñoz. When this church started a few years ago, it was meeting in a garage where the sanctuary measured nine by twelve feet. The congregation kept knocking the back walls down until they were meeting in a little larger sausage-shaped sanctuary. The church built a small building and then later began to meet at a movie theater that was known for its risqué films. The church workers needed to cover the upcoming movie ads with brown paper since the congregation could only rent the place two days a week. Soon, however, it became seven days a week, twenty-four hours a day until church growth forced a move to a large factory, shed-like building. This means that the heat beats through the makeshift roof in the summer, and the cold seeps in miserably during the winter. When it rains the sewers back up into the church, bringing along an unpleasant smell. In spite of these inconveniences, the church has expanded to more than one thousand in attendance in these few years, and they have now purchased a larger property nearby so they can build again to accommodate the people.

Pastor Edgardo has a very telling series of comments concerning how to pastor a revival and stay away from fads, extremes, or heresy. "As far as our local church goes," he says, "we have seen the hand of God in a very special way, and we have been a part of all kinds of things. For example, we have had meetings where people would spontaneously fall down laughing or weeping along with other unusual events, but we have always been open. In the churches that attempted to force things, there have been problems and in the churches that tried to put a stop to it, there also were problems."[5]

"We simply accept everything that God does," Pastor Edgardo continued, "but we try to place a great deal of emphasis on the sediment that remains after each wave of revival. There may be people very touched by the Lord, but our responsibility is that those people be transformed into good Christians. Therefore we need a strong emphasis on teaching. More than 20 percent of our church is involved in some type of ministerial training."[3]

Lately there has been a strong emphasis in the church concerning the nations. The goal is that a very high percentage of the church's income will be used for missions and that some day they can send out more income than what remains within the church. At this point the church generally sends almost 30 percent of its income out to missions, to our fellowship, or to new church plants.[6]

Until the End

God's will is for His church to live in revival, and for this to happen we need good pastors. Stagnation was never in His plan. Non-productive years where there are no surprises and no risks taken are anathema to Him. We must continually sow the seeds of faith that produce long-lasting revivals in growing, healthy churches across the nation and around the world until Jesus comes to take us all to that fabulous celebration supper.

God, give us a heart to pastor the revival long-term. We want to see even more come to find Jesus as their Lord and disciple them into maturity!

6

Young Evangelists

IN THIS REVIVAL, as in many others in history, the Holy Spirit has chosen to use young evangelists to touch lives, and it is amazing to witness. Many of them have had contact with recognized ministries, but they are not photocopies or echoes of someone else's burden. Each has a special touch of the Spirit.

Those of us who have been around for a while have enjoyed watching the younger generations arise and grow strong. As they spend time seeking God in their early years, they are preparing their hearts and lives. I have observed the anointing coming upon them and the boldness arise.

Once we had a visitor from the U.S. who was praying for our students. She works in a similar setting and has prayed for many Bible college students in her time. Suddenly she stepped back and said, "As I pray, I sense that so many of these young people are going to be such strong evangelists. I feel their boldness and sometimes while I pray for them, I have had pictures of the places in which they will be ministering. They are in huge stadiums... and preaching to thousands of people. In all of my time in the United States, I haven't prayed for this many strong evangelists. It shakes me up. It is wonderful!"

Indeed the Lord seems to be raising up a strong, new generation. There are so many stories.

DANTE GEBEL

When Dante was sixteen years old, his European immigrant pastor shook a crooked finger in his face and said to him, "Dante, God will never use you." But thankfully, Dante listened to the Dreammaker, Jesus Christ, and not to the dreamsquasher. By his twenty-eighth birthday in the year 2000, his life and ministry had touched over one million people.

Dante has his own program on Trinity Broadcasting Network (TBN) and has held youth gatherings in downtown Buenos Aires with 103,000 in attendance. God has used him to bring together more than eighty thousand young people at one time in the famous River Plate Stadium. He is an artist, actor, comedian, cartoonist, preacher, revivalist, and a raiser of the bar for the youth of today.

The other day in my class on Leviticus for Advanced Ministerial Training, we were commenting on the ethical trends of today and the common double standard, sometimes even in the church, concerning sexual experience previous to marriage. One pastor's comment made us all reflect with gratitude. "No one talked about the requirement of virginity previous to marriage applying to young men until Dante Gebel started talking about it," he said. "Now this stance is having its impact throughout the churches."

A secular newspaper stated that Dante is raising up an army of virgins. What a comment! It is unusual in a nation so given to sensuality. Sexual advertising is everywhere, and youth here sense such pressure to have name brand clothes. Anorexia and bulimia are major issues, as is depression among young people.

Was Dante perhaps an unlikely candidate? "God chooses the things that are not" (1 Cor. 1:28, author's paraphrase). Who exactly is this young man named Dante Gebel who dared to stem the tide?

He saw a vision of a stadium filled with thousands of young people. When he visited Claudio Freidzon's King of Kings Church, there was a prophecy stating that he was being raised up as a pastor for the youth of the nation of Argentina.

His biblical and theological training consists of night Bible school in IBE Morón, his own local church pastor, and being mentored by various pastors, including Claudio Freidzon. Much of his background and style were gleaned from the hundreds of preaching tapes from IBRP chapels that he checked out.

In 1991 God appeared to Dante and showed him as on a big screen a stadium full of young people. He reacted with trembling, fear, and a desire to run out of his room. He couldn't see who the preacher was, but he could tell it was a huge crowd of around seventy thousand young people.

A few months later he went to King of Kings Church and Claudio Freidzon prophesied: "What He said to you in the intimate and secret place now he makes public. He raises you up as the pastor of the youth of this nation." Various months after the prophecy, Dante asked his wife Liliana how it was going to come to pass. He felt like a failure as a youth leader in his church where many times he preached to only two people. He and Liliana realized that they didn't have money to rent a stadium as he had seen in his vision. "How are you going to preach in a stadium," she asked, "if no one knows you?" So during those first years of ministry they thought about the least expensive way to become known—the radio. Dante began to produce a radio program for youth that was full of humor, bite, and good music. His caricatures got people's attention at a time where there was much rigid legalism in the country. They had obtained the time on the radio they could afford, which was at 1 a.m. Within three months Dante would send these tapes free to up to two hundred fifty different radio stations and ended up being given time on one hundred eighty stations around the country.

Soon he was one of the best-known radio personalities

among the youth of Argentina. So he and Liliana thought, let's hold a crusade. At the time, the largest crowd of Christian young people that could be gathered was five thousand for a rock group. Dante's picture in his vision early in the morning in 1991 had been of a stadium full of seventy thousand youths, which was unheard of at the time.

The first crusade had five thousand in attendance and the second had six thousand. This still was a long way from the seventy thousand he had seen. For the third crusade, he felt led of God to rent a soccer stadium. He began to announce on his weekly television broadcast that he had reserved the Velez Sarsfield Stadium, which holds sixty-five thousand. The story of that major jump is one of God's coordination of some of the most diverse characters.

As the date of the encounter grew near, the stadium officials called and informed him that if he didn't come up with at least half of the rental money by the next Monday, they would scuttle his rental agreement and hold a soccer game on that day. In distress, he went to church that Friday night. No one knew of the challenge of faith he was in, but that evening a lady in the congregation had a word from God for him: "The answer is yours tonight before midnight." He hurried home to make it before the midnight hour—yes, that is how it is during revival—and the phone rang at fifteen minutes to midnight.

"Dante Gebel? I'd like to ask you a couple of questions." The man then slowly and deliberately rambled on, "Do you think God can use someone who has backslidden?"

As he tried to be polite to the man, he was thinking, "Get off the phone! God's answer has to reach me during these fifteen minutes."

"I watch your program," the man continued, "and you announced that you're inviting thousands of young people to an event at Velez Sarsfield stadium. Do you have the money for that event?"

Dante's answer of faith was "Why? We believe we will have the money."

"You don't look like you do," the man said. "How much do you need?"

"$60,000," Dante said.

"How would you like it? Small bills or large? Come by my office on Monday morning and get the money."

Not only did the man help him with the rental, but he invested another $15,000 in advertising and security.

The stadium was packed with fifty-five thousand young people seeking God. "The history of the youth of Argentina began to change there," Dante states. "The young people don't gather to seek healing or strange manifestations. They gather to celebrate a holy lifestyle. And they don't stay away from sin because of legalistic rules. They don't want to sin because they love God so much. As far as I'm concerned, that's revival."

For the next event, eighty thousand young people gathered. The one following had one hundred five thousand. At that gathering he challenged the politicians and government leaders who were watching on television: "Soon we will have a country without corruption in government and where the president does not go and consult witches."

In 1997 Dante participated in eighty-seven conferences, and then God told him that He had not asked Dante to do all those things, that his calling was a very specific one. So Dante cancelled everything on his agenda. For months one of the only invitations that he would agree to was to preach at River Plate Bible Institute.

During that time of prayer and waiting, God began to show him that many young people in the interior of the country couldn't make it to the large events he was holding, so he went to the provincial capitals and in different meetings where eight thousand or more would gather, many of whom had never been to a youth meeting of more than a couple hundred.

Dante's challenge? Don't preach to youth from a balcony

of holiness. Youth feel distanced from you. You have to come to their level and lead them to fall in love with Christ. When a youth gets anointed, it doesn't result in legalism like asking "How long should my skirt be?" It is more a living attitude born out, wanting to do what is best for others and for God.

Dante had to break through the typical church barriers regarding the youth crusades. Young people were showing up with their unsaved friends and that caused a clash in lifestyles. But this bold young evangelist was obedient to God and thousands of young people are living holy lives and serving God because he was.

ESTEBAN MACCIO

Esteban, a member of King of Kings Church, was one of the students who most sought God during his time of training at River Plate Bible Institute. While he could hear others playing volleyball, he was in the balcony of the chapel, receiving from the Holy Spirit. I remember the time God's power sent him backward fifteen feet over four rows of chairs into a group of students who were knocked down by the impact of his body.

He had just graduated and was wondering how God would be using his life. Then a trip to Europe to minister had come together very quickly.

Esteban called me from Europe. "I preached on the streets and in the bars in Switzerland. That is unusual there, and I talked to many people who had never heard about Jesus. Once a plain-clothes police officer was communicating to the chief of police by walkie-talkie and repeating what I was saying on the street. 'He says that Jesus loves you.'" Interesting way for the chief of police to hear the gospel.

Esteban went to a bar where all the drug addicts gather and asked the owner for permission to preach. The wife of the owner, who was trembling because of the lack of drugs, gave her life to Christ. He preached fifty-two times in two months and the village council of a city in Switzerland offered to pay for his trip back so he can continue to preach against drugs.

On a subsequent trip to Europe he was invited to speak at a private high school where students live on campus. God used him to reveal the sins of two hundred of the some five hundred students, calling them to repentance. The amazing aspect of this sign is that he sang the words of knowledge from God's Spirit, and his translator merely spoke the phrases. Some manifested demons and were set free in the middle of Europe! Hearts received those prophetic words and every student went forward from his seat, most of them weeping as they surrendered to Christ.

Marcela Acosta

When Marcela Acosta was a student at River Plate Bible Institute, she would often give testimony in chapel on Monday, the day when time is provided for students to share. Each week we would hear her state things like "Four accepted Christ on the train" or "This weekend six people gave their lives to Christ."

Marcela and a girlfriend would board the train at rush hour when it is packed with people. She would begin to preach using her testimony: "I had suffered so much when I was a teenager that I didn't want to live anymore. I had no hope. Four different times I attempted to take my own life. Then I met someone who changed my life completely. He gave me hope and a reason to live. If you are feeling that your life is full of sadness or if you have lost hope, He can help you, too. His name is Jesus Christ."

Today Marcela and her husband are planting a church in Madrid, Spain.

Damián González

"The cross made a dividing line in my life," Damián González shared with a group of young people visiting from the United

States. "Before, I was a drug addict and a drug dealer. I weighed less than one hundred pounds, didn't eat much, and had lost relationship with my family. I thought I was HIV positive, and my goal was simply to live to my twenty-first birthday.

"One morning at six o'clock, Satan came into my room," Damián continued. "I felt the flames of hell. I started crying out for help from a woman of prayer, my mother. When she came into my room, she asked, 'Are you willing to accept Jesus as your personal Saviour?' I answered, 'Where do I sign?' That day the cross of Jesus changed my life."

One of Damián's first thoughts when his parents took him to church was "I want that pulpit!" A call to preach was already stirring in his heart. He began to try to share his faith with anyone he encountered, but he was seeing few results. Realizing that he needed more of the right tools to minister, he left his home in Rosario, moving to Buenos Aires in 1997 to enter River Plate Bible Institute.

During his freshman year as he was sitting in one of my evangelism classes, he wrote in large letters on his notebook, "Lord, make me an evangelist." He also made a covenant with God that he would not let a day go by during which he did not witness to at least one unbeliever concerning his faith in Christ.

Excited about the effective tools he was receiving at school to communicate the gospel, he put them to use constantly. He would stand on the bus stop corner and ask how to get to the neighborhood of the Bible school, though he knew full well. As people would give him directions they would say, "You're not from here, are you? Where are you from?" And finally they would ask, "What brings you here to Buenos Aires?" In his heart, Damián would think, *This is my opportunity!* and he would share his testimony and his call. Most of these individuals would pray with him to receive Christ.

One day he walked up to three young men in a park as they were smoking marijuana. His attempts to share with them were mocked and rebuffed. Suddenly a tinge of righteous indignation came on him, and he exclaimed, "Tell you what. I'm going to pray for you guys in the name of Jesus and if nothing happens to you, I'll quit preaching this gospel for the rest of my life. I'll sit right down here and smoke marijuana with you." They accepted the proposition and soon Damián was praying for all he was worth.

"Lord, thank You for all You have done for these young men. They have hurt Your heart with their lifestyles, but You went to the cross and died for each of them. I ask You to touch them right now and show them how much You love them." Suddenly the young men began to shake and to weep. Of course, Damián is still preaching the gospel.

During his freshman year of Bible school he began to receive invitations to preach all over the country. But when he arrived back at his church, his pastor told him to cancel them all and to stay in his local church. For two months no opportunity was afforded him there. Then one day the pastor said he could take a little wooden platform and some chairs if he wanted to hold a neighborhood campaign somewhere.

Damián chose his own neighborhood and he began preaching, asking forgiveness of his friends and neighbors for fomenting drug addiction and delinquency and for selling drugs in the neighborhood. In that three-day event, more than one hundred of his neighbors accepted Christ.

As he was preaching one of those evenings, a dance band of many of his friends walked by playing drums. One of his buddies yelled mockingly at him, "Hey, *chufli,* why don't you leave drugs and grab the Bible?" Damián stopped his speaking and spoke directly to the group. "You're all smiles on the outside now, but then you get home and you are totally alone. I was that way for a long time. But I met the Creator of life and He has given me life. If you come up here and accept Him today, He will transform your life, too."

Of the thirty-eight young people in the band, nineteen

went forward to accept Jesus. The young man who yelled insultingly at him is now a Bible school student!

Damián asked permission of his pastor to train a team of evangelists, and received approval. To his surprise, however, no one in the church wanted to learn how to reach lost people. When he prayed about this, he sensed the Holy Spirit saying to him, "You want a team of evangelists? Go out and win them." So he did; fifty of them. And soon he had them trained to go to the hospitals, the AIDS wards, and parks.

He would often get on a bus with his some of his team, and they would talk with the people. Once he sensed God telling him that a certain woman was a prostitute and that he should speak to her. At first he thought, *I don't want to be seen with a prostitute.* However, he was obedient to what God wanted and sat down next to her, saying, "You suffered quite a bit when you were a child, right?"

"How do you know?" she answered.

"Because God is telling me and He also wants you to know how much He loves you." Soon she was weeping and accepted Christ as Savior, along with five people around her who had overheard the conversation.

In Argentina one of the most important holidays to spend with family is Christmas Eve. The idea is to eat together and raise a toast at midnight. Soon Damián was out with his team in the plazas or hospitals on that very evening, sharing Christ's love. People got healed in the hospital wards. Then in one of the parks he found a homeless man and invited him to the house for Christmas Eve dinner. Damián considers his mother a saint for accepting some of the people he has taken home. That evening they decided to help the man clean up, and his mother began to unwind the bandages off the man's feet and to wash them. As she ran gauze between the toes, maggots fell out!

Once a doctor called saying that he was treating a woman who thought God was going to heal her so she had not received medical help for a year. The woman was dying of cancer and had only days to live. It was amazing that this professional man of the traditional religion should be asking: Would Damián come and pray for her? Damián went to the hospital where the woman was pale and slumped in a wheelchair. Her thirty-five-year-old daughter was there along with her doctor. He talked about the power of God and then prayed for her. She was instantly and permanently healed! He turned and led the daughter to the Lord and then the doctor. He started prophesying over the doctor: "God has chosen you as an instrument of honor. The day will come that you will not heal by medicine but by the power of God." That doctor is now an active member in the local church, serving God through medical practice and seeing many divine healings through his own ministry.

Damián's spirit is contagious. He preaches with passion and lives passionately what he preaches. He has challenged and trained hundreds of young people to reach out with real love to the lost.

One night a group of us, including Damián, were returning late after a service and just made it into Burger King before they closed at one o'clock. We were all sitting down to eat our hamburgers and fries when Damián disappeared. We noticed his food getting cold and wondered where he was. After quite a while, he came down from the bathroom upstairs, which had been temporarily closed for repairs. He had been leading the plumber to Christ. It was a very timely witness in that the plumber's wife had passed away that very week. "My food is to do the will of Him who sent Me" (John 4:34, NKJV). Sounds familiar.

SERGIO ABREGÚ

Sergio Abregú was leading a rather uneventful life through his freshman year at River Plate Bible Institute. Then he received the baptism in the Holy Spirit and his life radically changed. At that moment he promised God that he would do anything the Holy Spirit led him to do.

Suddenly, despite still being a student in Bible college, he was getting invitations to speak in various churches. On one of those occasions he was preaching in a church of about fifty people that seemed extremely rigid and dry. He sensed the Holy Spirit telling him to announce that it was going to rain there. So he obeyed and then wondered how that was going to happen. The Spirit told him to get a bucket of water and pour it on the people. When the pastor had the bucket brought in, Sergio flung the water on the people and each place the water fell the people broke out praising God in tongues. The pastor asked for another bucket of water and was pointing to some of the corners of the small auditorium saying, "Pour some over there!"

In his senior year at Bible school he was asked to hold a series of meetings in his own local church in the Buenos Aires suburb of Hurlingham. On one of the nights of the campaign he was praying for the sick when a lady and her daughter were riding by in a car. Since the church did not have the funds to put windows in yet, the sound carried easily out to the street. "What's going on there?" the lady asked her daughter.

"It is an evangelical church, and they're praying for the sick," was her daughter's retort.

"Stop the car; I'm going in there!" the lady exclaimed. As she was walking down the aisle, the Holy Spirit communicated to Sergio that she could not see, but that she would be healed.

"What is your need?" asked Sergio.

"I'm blind, and I want to be healed," she answered. The young evangelist prayed and soon the lady was running up and down the aisle of the church yelling, "I can see! I can see!"

On another occasion, God's Spirit told Sergio to pour oil in the ear of a young lady. As soon as he did so, her perforated eardrum was healed!

During his very first years of ministry, Sergio was asked to speak at a gathering of six hundred youth leaders. The idea was for the leadership to get to know him and determine whether they wanted him to speak at their united youth convention. As he was going up to the platform the person coordinating the service said, "You have half an hour and don't mention the Holy Spirit."

But the Spirit of God said, "You'll speak as long as I tell you to and about what I determine." He spoke for an hour about the Person of the Holy Spirit and four hundred of the leaders received the infilling. The majority of the leaders wanted to have him speak at the upcoming youth convention, and over six thousand youth attended with four hundred of them accepting Christ as their Savior.

For the senior missions trip of his graduating class from River Plate Bible Institute, we all went to Honduras. God used the students greatly. Both Sergio and Damián were in the same class. While in Honduras, Sergio received an invitation to return for an evangelistic tour. When he arrived, he was ministering to fifty. Sergio stayed and presently he is helping to pastor twenty thousand youth. God has given him open doors to the people in high places in the government, and the Word is affecting many lives there. Sergio's ministry has touched the lives of scores of students in 115 schools all over Honduras.

NATHAN GRAMS

Our son, Nathan, is one of the young evangelists God has touched deeply here in Argentina. From the time he was ten years old he has sensed a missionary call. Even at that age, he and his close friend, Fernando Vena, would walk almost ten kilometers to Guernica, a very poor neighborhood, where they were in charge of a boys' Christian training program. Nathan shows such freshness in his interpretation of the Word. Let me share from my journal concerning some key moments in this young minister's life.

November 24, 1996:

Sam Hinn had a very special word for Sherry and me. Later, he told me that at times he sensed my heaviness. What he stated was that God had our tears and our sorrows registered and that they would produce fruit. Then he said that Nathan is a preacher and also a worshiper and that God had given him something very special that his generation would need a great deal.

May 18, 1997:

At long last I'm writing again. So much has happened— so much is missed. Nathan's three-day fight with nightmares and oppression, then how God used him to heal two people of flat feet.

July 2, 1997

Nathan has really been used of the Lord during these last few days. He's been trembling in the Spirit, weeping and laughing, but so quietly. Edgardo rearranged things so he could speak in church tonight, and he told me that God had let him know this morning that he'd be speaking tonight. What a beautiful time in the Lord!

July 10, 1997

God is doing some special things through Sergio Scataglini and through Nathan—He keeps surprising us.

August 24, 1997

This weekend Nathan spoke five times and turned one time down. God did some very special things at the Belgrano (King of Kings) church retreat he spoke for at the Bible School.

These sorts of stirrings and ministry opportunities kept happening for our son. Presently he is in the United States attached as an associate pastor to Emmanuel Christian Center, a large church in Minneapolis, where he is ministering to a congregation of Hispanics and other internationals. He has organized large crusades and outreaches and is constantly seeing people come to Christ.

ELIANA NERVEGNA

During her teenage years, pastor's daughter Eliana Nervegna decided to rebel. She not only exchanged church for the discotheque, she also took most of the youth group with her. As she was dancing one day, God called her. He let her know how much He loved her and that He was going to use her to reach people all over the world for His kingdom. Weeping as she continued to dance, she accepted the call. Soon she was enrolled as a student at River Plate Bible Institute.

When Eliana came to her senior year, God placed on her heart a vision to unite the young people of her area by holding a prayer meeting at the Merlo Plaza on November 27, 1999. The emphasis was to ask forgiveness as a city and ask for the blessing of God. When she approached the pastors' association with the idea, they informed her that a youth leader had been struggling with the same proposal but had never presented it because he was afraid. The day Eliana came forward with the same plan, he thought he would work with her because it was evident that God was leading. This event would cost ten thousand dollars, so they said when she could raise the first three thousand dollars toward it, they would realize that God was in it. For a young lady who has no job and is in training, that sum seemed impossible, but God miraculously provided the funds and the permission from the municipality. This seemed impossible since the place chosen to gather was a main avenue that had never been cut off to traffic, much less for an evangelistic event. The city also provided security and the required ambulances.

As the day was approaching, rain was forecast. It had rained every day that week. The youth leadership of the different churches were calling her at home to ask if the event would be cancelled because of the weather. She quickly placed a greeting on her answering service that stated, "The event will be held. Tomorrow is going to be a beautiful, sunny day." That was the case, one of the nicest October days we have had.

At the plaza six thousand young people had gathered and at a certain moment Eliana asked them all to kneel and pray, asking forgiveness for the city. Of the crowd, four hundred accepted the Lord and two hundred entered Christian drug rehabilitation programs.

Today Eliana is traveling to different parts of the world, preaching the gospel and affecting many lives for the kingdom, just as God promised.

FERNANDO PATALAGOITIA

Each year, on New Year's Eve from the time he was fourteen years old until he was sixteen, Fernando and his friends would celebrate by going out to steal a car. He gave his life to Jesus after seeing the miracles in his family. His father was an alcoholic and his parents were on the verge of divorce, when God healed their marriage and plucked his dad out of alcoholism.

Fernando was baptized and entered IBRP. "Here God turned my life around, and His fire gave me a growing love for souls," he states.

Today, the former delinquent takes groups of young people to the hospital to pray for the sick. Now on the thirty-first of December, they spend some time with their families and then go to the hospital to pray for people until one o'clock. The sick are being healed and lonely people are receiving God's love.

One day in an open-air evangelistic impact a witch appeared. Before Fernando could start preaching, the woman wanted to beat him up but held back crying out: "I am being invaded!" Fernando answered: "God loves you, and you need to repent." Her answer was, "I am with the demons!" God protected the young evangelist by His power, and the woman began to back away and then walked off muttering insults. After that episode many people were impacted by the gospel.

Oscar Benitez

Oscar Benítez, a young missionary evangelist, shared recently in chapel in IBRP. He had been visiting the different Argentine missionaries in thirteen different countries and prayed one day: "Lord, I would like to plant a church. I'm getting tired of traveling so much." God led him to Monterrey, Mexico where he thought, *I need some type of means of support.* So he drew from his experience as a young Bible school student when for a time he had worked in a bakery. He opened an "Argentine bakery" where bread and rolls that are everyday occurrences here became the rage. Hundreds of people became delighted customers.

At the same time Oscar began services just above the bakery. God began to do signs and wonders, including many deliverances from demonic possession with the accompanying physical manifestations.

People lined up on the ground floor to buy bread and pastries would be startled constantly by the activities on the second floor. "This is not the best publicity for a bakery," he thought and determined to rent a different building for the church.

Since its beginnings in February of 2004 this congregation has grown to several hundred people in attendance. Healings are common in the new church. God is at work in Mexico!

They Keep Arriving on the Scene

Andrés Ghioni is presently in training. His uncle, a well-known evangelist, was also a student at River Plate Bible Institute and was a man who prayed for hours when he was a student. Most weekends Andrés is seeing the power of God demonstrated to heal. He preaches healing campaigns constantly. Some of the illnesses healed include: arthritis, diabetes, asthma, hernias, epilepsy, deafness, pneumonia, ulcers, allergies, hemiplegia, and issue of blood. Andy has also seen people freed of demon possession in his campaigns.

Young evangelist Andrés gives this testimony: "In a campaign in the city of Moreno as one of the meetings was drawing to a close the assistant pastor called me aside and asked me to pray for a t-shirt that someone had brought that belonged to a needy loved-one. I prayed and went home. A few days later, as I was traveling with the same assistant pastor, the topic of the t-shirt came up and the man told me that it belonged to a paralyzed man who was prostrate in bed. When the t-shirt was placed on the man's body, fire began to burn him and he got up from the bed and began to run around the house. That is when he realized that God had healed him."

In Santiago del Estero, Andrés went to visit a man who was skin and bones. The man told the young evangelist that he just wanted to die. As they conversed, the Holy Spirit let Andy know that the man was being tormented by an evil spirit that cooperated with the sickness and that he should cast it out. In his own words: "I placed my hands on him and cast the evil spirit out. Then I asked him how he felt and he said that he realized that "something" had left him. A few months later, I found out that he had gained sixteen kilograms (thirty-five pounds) and that he had been healed. Glory to God."

Héctor Ferreyra's son, Nicolás, is a student presently and out on every weekend preaching healing and evangelistic campaigns. He has a vision to hold a large youth crusade in every southern province in Argentina. He is somewhat shy personally, but when he stands up with a microphone and starts ministering, there is a mighty boldness and power of God upon him.

This year the students worked together to plant a church, and, in a matter of two months, they already have twelve cell groups going plus cell groups for prostitutes and others for transvestites. The church meets in the plaza twice a week and is pastored by Gustavo Guex, another young evangelist. They sing for a while, and then Gustavo stands up on a park table and begins to preach. People gather and other Bible school students go around and share the gospel. Recently when I visited, there was a poor couple who came forward to accept Christ at the end, along with an old man with one leg. There was a well-to-do and distinguished man who was touched along with a boy who had just been shooting up drugs. He fell under the power of God when Pastor Gustavo prayed for him. Three children accepted Christ and then there was the prostitute who hung out along the sides but got ministered to by one of our young ladies.

God's process goes on! We're not sure what they will all become, but there are many more young people now, praying and earnestly seeking the Lord. God is giving them dreams. Developing are Christian David Albert, Erick Riveros, Mónica Obando, Lucas López, Leo Campbell, Karolina Zacarías— and so many more. May the Lord give them the keys that will keep the revival going into their generation.

7

Keys to Revival

We Americans are very "fix-it" oriented. Give us a problem, and we'll locate a person who can move onto the scene and make things happen. We'll find a how-to book or an expert who is the best in that particular field and then the situation will get resolved. We're trouble-shooters and go-getters. Need to cap an ocean-floor petroleum spill? We'll find a way. Need to find the sunken Titanic? We can do it. Want to have a nice icy treat on a summer day? An eleven-year-old developed the popsicle. Parking meters, the escalator, Kool-Aid, potato chips, blue jeans, Silly Putty, tractors, bar codes, the microwave oven, Fountain pens, crayons, eyeglasses, Q-tips, the vacuum cleaner, motorcycles, and the electric iron—all from a very inventive people, prolific in creativity and accustomed to getting the job done.

Unfortunately, this can-do perspective does not work well with God's grace and His sovereign design. An awakening is His doing. Revival is up to Him. Our systems will only tend to alienate the Holy Spirit's deep working in our lives. "Like a dove" carries a lot of meaning. All of our intensity in planning, budgeting, charting, and wishful thinking will not get Him to speak, let alone act.

In other words, there is no paint by number revival kit. One cannot come up with the elements humanly, give a little clap of the hands, and "Poof!" produce a move of God. When we turn over to God all of our ingredients—our time, energy, our very selves—then many times He surprises us with a distinct moving deep within our being and then through us out to others. Though God likes it when we seek Him, praying a certain number of hours per day, lying on our faces before God, and telling Him a thousand times that we want revival will not work by itself. The truth is that nothing will work besides casting ourselves on God's gracious mercy.

It should not be a surprise that this chapter is not a man-made, time-tested formula for revival. It is a description of some of the ingredients that God uses in His own recipe for revival, when He wants to send it—which is usually today, right now, if we will just let Him. God's grace is so amazing.

BROKENNESS

My pastor, Cyril Homer, used to say, "A man or a woman is not really ready to be a leader until he or she goes down to the bottom with God." The training school for revival pastors has been the school of brokenness.

Claudio and Betty Freidzon had seven years of desert with very few people in their church before God began to give their ministry an increase. They would show a series of films on Jesus in the Parque Chas neighborhood near Belgrano, their present location. People would watch from halfway across the park, but as soon as the lights came on, they would disappear into the shadows. Altar calls seemed to fall on deaf ears.

One day Claudio got a great idea. "Betty," he said to his wife, "Right at the end of the film, I'll go up front and be ready to give the call to accept Christ. You switch on the lights, and I'll start to speak immediately. That way no one will have a chance to get away." All to no avail; there was no fruit.

Once Claudio became so discouraged that he decided to quit the ministry. God intervened, however, with an encouraging word from their superintendent at just the right time.

Thank God, they stayed and walked through their valley of brokenness together.

Pedro Ibarra, who today is a well-known revival pastor in Quilmes, Buenos Aires, pastored five little old ladies for five years in a church with a difficult history. Pastor Ibarra fasted, prayed, sought God, tried everything he knew, and experienced no growth. Now, of course, it is entirely different, but five difficult years seems like a long time when you're in it.

Guillermo Prein had a similar experience. He preached twelve times a day on the street and once at night for the first six months at the beginning of that church plant in Parque Patricios. Not one person accepted Christ! But the owner of the vineyard had promised him that there would be much fruit, and today they have one thousand seven hundred cell groups and twenty-six thousand people attending church with water baptisms each quarter averaging over four hundred.

We have to die out to ourselves. "Most assuredly, I say to you, unless a grain of wheat falls into the ground and dies, it remains alone; but if it dies, it produces much grain" (John 12:24, NKJV). Dying doesn't feel good, but real fruit doesn't come without it. The increase of these churches is due to the brokenness of the pastors and their willingness to die.

DESPERATION

Besides going through the school of brokenness, these pastors who are being used so mightily in the revival have all evidenced a strong hunger for more of God. Sergio Scataglini went after God with such desperation that he said, "Take me home or give me a revelation of yourself." When the answer came, it transformed the course of the ministry for him and his wife, Kathy.

We could go through a list of men and women who have been mightily used of the Lord in this revival and a key characteristic is evident in each of their lives. All of them were desperate to know the Person of the Holy Spirit. They were not willing to settle for the natural, for business-as-usual ministry or Christianity. They were hungry—not for change or to be more useful or to have a broader ministry—but for God Himself.

A former dean of River Plate Bible Institute, Brother Verner Kniessel, visited Claudio Freidzon in 1992. Claudio and Betty's church had begun to blossom, and Claudio was happy to tell his former teacher, college administrator, and friend about his entire weekly schedule, including a nightly radio broadcast at midnight.

Brother Verner heard him out and then asked a simple question that shook Claudio's life. "When do you have time for the Holy Spirit?" That question hit home and stayed with him constantly. Soon after that Pastor Pedro Ibarra loaned him Benny Hinn's book, *Good Morning, Holy Spirit*. Claudio was so intrigued with the evident personal relationship that Brother Hinn had with the Holy Spirit that he decided to go visit him at his church.

Traveling to the United States was an enormous undertaking for a pastor of a church of any size back in those difficult days. The church prayed and Claudio traveled to where Benny was holding revival services. His persistence, his sacrificial investment of funds, and time away from his church all points to a desperation that pleased God.

I was speaking for a couples' encounter at a retreat center just after Claudio returned from that trip. He asked to take a walk with me and shared the prophecy Benny Hinn had spoken concerning his ministry, that he would be traveling and preaching in Europe and all over the world. At the time, it seemed so far-fetched and incredible, but I listened. Since then I have often had occasion to think of those prophecies as I have looked at the videos in Rey de Reyes Church of Claudio's trips and listened to his accounts of meetings in Europe, Africa, Asia, and North America. God chose a man who sought Him without reservation. Desperation is so real—and it is impossible to imitate.

It was desperation for God that drove Pastor Alberto Scataglini, Sergio's father, to pray with the youth of his church for months, seeking revival. The answer came from the Lord through the ministry of Evangelist Carlos Annacondia. What a time! There were eight months of campaign with the participation of seven churches at first, then most of the churches in the city joined in. God moved mightily and forty thousand and fifty thousand people made decisions for Christ.

When Pastor Omar Olier's wife, Graciela, received God's refreshing through the revival and began to minister powerfully to people, Omar was not present. His first decision when he saw what the Lord had given his wife was to go and seek the same outpouring. At first, nothing happened as he sought and prayed all night. But then at seven o'clock, the Lord poured out a cataract of love and power on him. Their church in Mar del Plata has grown from three to eight thousand presently.[1] Dozens of pastors look to him for spiritual leadership. Conferences and evangelistic thrusts in Singapore and India along with much fruit in many cities and small towns of Argentina date back to the time they took to seek all that God had for them and their church. I wonder what would have happened (or not happened, is the better question) if he had not spent time to seek God.

Missionary to Argentina Steve Hill also spent months seeking God with total abandon when he lived and worked in Neuquén, in southern Argentina. Prayer, the Word, and reading books by Robert Murray McCheyne and Leonard Ravenhill filled his life. I clearly remember a luncheon barbeque at the Southern Cone Missionary Retreat where we all looked forward to the amazing array of different cuts of beef, pork, and chicken. As I entered the dining hall I noticed Steve sitting outside the doors with a glass of water in his hand. "Aren't you joining us for the *asado*?" I asked. The answer amazed me. He was fasting that day. The Lord was putting down the foundation for what was ahead. Although God did much through his ministry and his wife Jeri's here in Argentina, the answer to Steve's search and total commitment came on Father's Day four years later in Pensacola, Florida. That was the beginning of the Brownsville Revival.

Recently over a cup of coffee I asked Pastor Osvaldo Carnival what his greatest frustration was. With a church of fifteen thousand to pastor it would have been easy to talk about some church problem or a certain type of person or something they needed to see changed in the church. That's why his answer was so memorable. "I have a kind of holy frustration to desire more," he said. "I know I'm a beloved son, but I just want more. I yearn to give more of myself to God." All of us at the table felt our emotions leap into our throats as we sensed this pastor's intense hunger for God.

Youth Evangelist Dante Gebel has been used by God to bring together ninety-eight thousand young people at one time here in Buenos Aires to celebrate before the Lord and to make a public commitment to holiness. One of the keys to his ministry's fruitfulness has been the fact that a little old lady called him every morning at six o'clock to pray. He also often spends the night in prayer until the dawn.

Prayer

People down through revival history have committed themselves to time for prayer. William Seymour is reported to have spent hours praying at the Azusa Street Mission with his head buried between two wooden milk crates. Frank Bartleman, at that time, had such a burden for the work that his wife feared for his life. His prayer and fasting accompanied by missed sleep was so intense. Count Zizendorf prayed so much that a prayer meeting finally kicked off amongst the Moravians on his estate, which lasted one hundred years, every day, twenty-four-hours per day. The stories go on.

Here in Argentina, prayer becomes a way of life. Pastor Carnival calls it "the breathing mechanism of the believer." It is not done to twist God's arm to do something, but because people love spending time in His presence.

A few months back, one of our students Mariana Gonzalez Crotti, who is married to one of our graduates and is the mother of several small children, asked my opinion about a vision she had experienced. She sensed that people would be praying and interceding for the nation in the Plaza de Mayo, which is the city's main square. Recently, there had been some big demonstrations there with people beating on pans and confronting police. She said she felt God wanted her to do something to help make the vision become a reality, so I recommended that she obey the Holy Spirit.

She mentioned this to her pastor and to an IBRP student, which mustered forces for about thirty to go down to the plaza in a dilapidated bus each evening. They prayed for a few nights, marching around the main plaza right in front of the Rose House National Government Building. Unbeknownst to them, a national media network picked this up and some of the students were filmed praying. There was a very clear and beautiful prayer of intercession for the nation that was aired.

This motivated other Christians. Pastor Claudio Freidzon saw it on TV and felt that others should get involved. For weeks hundreds of pastors from Buenos Aires had been meeting regularly to pray. They sent out a mass e-mail to the churches to join them in prayer at the Plaza de Mayo. Literally thousands gathered together and kneeled in the Plaza where they interceded for the country, repented, prayed the Lord's Prayer together, and sang "Heal Our Nation." Visions do come true.

Previous to the 2001 social crisis, up to seventy pastors and their wives of many different denominations met together for fellowship. Gathered in a restaurant, they were surprised by the television images of a social uprising. In Pastor Pedro Ibarra's words, "People were burning cars, breaking windows, and stealing." The police would not intervene; they only stood by as spectators. Everything culminated in the government's collapse and that fatal day, twenty-seven people died and there were a multitude of wounded.

Seeing that situation, the pastors gathered and decided to lift an altar of prayer for the nation. During those days, there was a prophetic word stated that if an altar was not raised for the nation, blood would flow in the streets. The convocation was from God.

During those first months, more than 1,200 pastors participated. The central focus was not preachers or personalities. The central focus was prayer. God answered that plea and that evil was detained. The nation entered into a stage of social and economic restoration and into a much different stability.[2] Hundreds of pastors continued to gather weekly for prayer during the next two and a half years.

It is difficult to get leaders of the revival to talk about their personal prayer lives, but I happen to know that Claudio Freidzon spent six hours a day in prayer—and that at the height of the revival when he was busy with just a few other things. I also know he fasted during the entire week of sanctification held at the church recently. As he drove, he would speak in tongues for two hours at a time.

Now at Rey de Reyes there is a six o'clock prayer meeting twice a week attended by one hundred to one thousand people. The whole church shows up for the two special weeks of prayer and fasting and for the week of sanctification that they have every year—more attendance than even for a special visiting speaker.

Another smaller church that I know, just had a meeting of their intercession group, and forty to fifty men and women showed up. They are committed to prayer, and a one-hour meeting turned into three and a half. A pastor once called the weeks of prayer emphasis in his church a "lab." It is the place where believers can learn to listen to God, to know His voice, and to get direction for their lives and ministry.

A Chinese Presbyterian church of Buenos Aires spends each Friday night in prayer. The entire night is a combination of praise, worship, and prayer. Many other churches dedicate a full night per month to a "vigil or prayer" celebration.

Catedral de la Fe also has prayer week emphases as well as a week of sanctification every year. The last one was so packed that they had to have the youth sit on the platform and floors. People are changed as they seek God.

Pastor Carnival shared about prayer in his life, discussing the importance of this discipline. "Every time I come out of prayer," he said, "I get new impressions and fresh visions. Once I was praying earnestly about whether God wanted us to be on secular television. I sensed He did, but I couldn't imagine how that would work. Then in prayer I felt God speaking to me through Acts 12 and Peter's imprisonment, saying that He can open any door, even ones that men and angels can't open. Shortly after that I met an important man who got me in touch with the owner of a TV channel, and we were soon on secular television."

Prayer in the individual lives of the leaders as well as in the church routine is an inherent part of what God is doing in Argentina. These stories abound.

PAIN

So many have a powder-puff, romanticized idea of what revival is. "Let's get together and sing choruses for a few hours, and God will do some signs and wonders," we might think. Although many times revival is living a taste of what Heaven will be, much of it has to do with excruciating pain, in the spiritual realm as well as emotionally and physically.

The anointing is total commitment-type stuff. It takes

everything we have all the time. And although it is exciting to see God work, to watch the fruit come in, to be surprised time and again by His Spirit, those who have been used in this revival have been in up to their necks—all of the time.

Our hobby for a few years now has been worship and prayer. Our strength has been renewed in the presence of the Lord. Pastors who have taken time to be together don't have any time at all for games and the latest video; they want to pray. It sounds grim and spartan, but willingness to live that lifestyle has been the prerequisite for survival.

There's a cost to the revival, and for quite a while you could tell a Pentecostal preacher here by the bleary eyes caused by lack of sleep, weeping, intense living, casting out demons, and ministering to people until the early hours of the morning.

When the La Plata campaign exploded in 1984, for months the workers and pastors slept in their clothes, no time even to change. They would get home from the campaign at three or four in the morning after praying for the demon-possessed and sick for hours on end. Revival isn't an extracurricular activity; it becomes the center around which the rest of life revolves.

Recently I was at the Hurlingham church with Héctor and Marga Manzolido, pastors of the revival. Since it was "Pastor's Day" I thought I would interview them a little before we honored them and prayed for them.

When I asked what their hobbies were, Héctor mentioned that he had none—that he thought he should, but that his life was the church. Marga mentioned that she was really good at crafts but had sensed in the midst of the revival that God was asking for her to give Him her hobby. She obeyed and hasn't touched a craft since. This was said with such easy abandon that it could not be mistaken for a new harsh legalism. It was a self-revealing testimony of her commitment to do nothing but be involved in what God is doing.

What does Paul mean when he says, "I put away childish things" (1 Cor. 13:11, NKJV)? They certainly love people and

God anyway and have put aside things so they are better able to show that love. Perhaps these pastors have a clearer idea, although it sounds rather strange to us with our schemes and diagrams of balance in the minister's life.

The cross caused Jesus enormous pain. Our daily cross should also. "Ye have not resisted unto blood" (Heb. 12:4) is a statement that comes to me quite often. How much do I really care? How comfortable do I need to be? What are my limits? My requirements? God have mercy.

TIME

God had worked in people's hearts, and I almost called them forward for prayer but then desisted and handed the service back to the associate pastor. It was Wednesday night, and I was on deputation. Sharing about the revival had been our joy. Many had listened with growing faith. I could tell they were thinking, "This is for me! I want to seek God for His moving in my life." What a precious moment in the presence of the Lord, and what anticipation was in my heart.

To my dismay, the associate pastor gave some quick announcements and dismissed the service. Before he and his wife took me out for a hamburger, one of the ladies of the church asked me why God didn't do the same mighty works in the United States. I answered that He does, but at camp or in the inner city, places where He is not put in a box.

As we were eating our hamburgers later, I mentioned to the brother that I felt badly that I hadn't called people forward for prayer. His answer still is etched on my memory, "We don't pray on Wednesday nights."

The tight schedule of activities and places did not allow for this congregation to give God time, on Wednesday nights anyway. Even if the Lord wanted to take over the schedule, it would be pretty hard. He'd almost have to immobilize people in authority so that the church could pray.

We were once invited to speak at a Missions Convention in the United States and were given exactly eight minutes to speak to the youth. That is a prime age to encourage them to serve God, but everything was orchestrated in a tight schedule by minutes. No time for God to move!

On another occasion we were supposed to minister to people in a prayer line. We wanted to take time to pray and the people seemed hungry for it, but the pastors pushed the people through. God had just a few minutes to get His blessing across to everyone.

I know we are not programmed for long services in the States, but maybe we should give God some margin to work with. Revival demands time.

"Where your treasure is, there will your heart be also" (Matt. 6:21). Jesus was so right about helping us evaluate where our priorities are. Just check the treasure investments: time, money, energy, thought life—that's our heart. Where are they? It is where the treasure is. And until our answers speak of giving God not just a portion, but all, revival will continue to tarry.

One of our guests to Argentina observed that here people's most meaningful relationships are in the church. Their heart is in the church, so their time is invested there also. Instead of trying to fit an hour or two of church per week into an already packed schedule, church members in Argentina look where they can put time for job and family into their church activities. Every holiday is spent in fellowship among the church family with special conferences and retreats often being held at these times. People say it is worth it because others are getting saved and the church is advancing. Plus, they're hungry for more themselves.

I remember a time when an ordained woman from the U. S., Dr. Carolyn Tennant, had preached in the morning at a women's conference in Mar del Plata, following which the ladies were supposed to have an afternoon off. Having ended on time (Argentine time), she then knelt on the floor because the power of God was so strong, finally collapsing in the Spirit for four hours. When she came to, the entire conference group was waiting, the auditorium still packed. They had been praying together over their churches, their provinces, and other countries for that whole time. The leader had said there would be a word from the Lord when she got up, and so they waited. Perhaps in the United States we would ask if it was going to be taped and not wait personally. She did have a word from the Lord, by the way, and at that conference everyone heard it for themselves.

The next day at these meetings she closed, saying that she was willing to pray for people if they desired. However, the conference was being held in a theater at a hotel where the seats were bolted down right up to the stage, leaving no room for altar space. She suggested that because of the situation, people minister to each other in their seats or wait there. But after she gave a general prayer and looked up, the entire group had formed a line stretching clear around the auditorium, and they waited for as long as five hours. The Spirit flowed in the gifts, with the worship team playing the entire time. When the line had ended, the musicians came down and asked for prayer, along with the video team, and some of the most meaningful ministry of the day occurred with these faithful workers. At the end of the evening service, people brought their friends and family to be prayed for and this continued until about two o'clock.

This type of hunger in Argentina is very impacting! People are so eager to hear from God. They are open and expectant, willing to wait on Him. Their anticipation seems to be rewarded by a mighty God who pours out upon them.

People are known to ride trains, buses, and walk, with the journeys sometimes taking hours, just to get to a church service or meeting they want to attend. They stand in lines wrapping around the block, waiting for hours sometimes to get into a church. They arrive very early just to be able to get a seat. Three or even five-hour services are not at all unusual here. No one seems to be in a hurry because the presence of God is there. Who would want to leave that?

The worship and praise goes on often for two or three hours before the preaching of the Word. God is there, and it is evident, almost palpable. Worship is not a shortened version of a few choruses to provide atmosphere, but a heartrending, life-changing few hours when people are changed, healed, and saved. There are no restrictions or artificial limits placed on the worship because people enjoy being with their Lord!

Spending time with God is not unique to Argentina or to the present time. Camp meetings, the brush arbor meetings of yesterday, tent crusades, all-night prayer vigils—these are the natural activities of a church wanting to be revived. We must give God time and do it because we want to seek Him, not as a bribe to receive the goods.

TRAVEL

To encourage each other and seek God together, the key people of this revival have been willing to travel, to go where the action is. "But tarry ye in the city of Jerusalem" (Luke 24:49). This was not an easy injunction for the disciples. Jerusalem was as challenging and foreign to them as Washington DC would be to someone from Cheyenne, Wyoming. It was the uncomfortable seat of political and religious power, but they obeyed. They found a way to be in one accord in the same geographical location and were suddenly surprised by the Holy Spirit's falling on them with tremendous power.

There were many hanging around, interested in Jesus' resurrection. Paul tells us that five hundred saw Jesus after His resurrection. Why then were only one hundred twenty waiting in the upper room when Pentecost fell? Some others probably decided that God could bless them wherever they were, going about their own business. They may have given Him permission to interrupt them in the ho-hum daily grind, but by not waiting in the appointed place with those who were willing to believe and commit time, they missed Pentecost.

It is likely that some others had started out with the group but then got tired and didn't wait the full ten days it took before the Holy Spirit moved upon them. That's a long time to wait around and pray, not knowing exactly what to expect. Would we give an undefined period of time to a prayer meeting, just waiting for something to happen in the future?

What a tremendous loss they must have felt, though, for the rest of their lives. "If I had only shown up to that ten-day prayer meeting. I understand the Spirit descended like a mighty wind, like fire on each of them, and that they were so impacted by the Holy Spirit that they acted drunk. I wish I had put off working in the fields for those ten days. I sure would have more to tell my grandchildren." What are all these days of our lives given to us for anyway?

One of the amazing aspects of this move of God in Argentina has been the willingness to go where God is moving. A demonstration of humility is that open, childlike attitude that says, "I want to see this. I'd like to be a part of that. I need that same touch on my life and ministry!"

When God shook the Rey de Reyes Church in Belgrano in 1993, people came to Buenos Aires from the provinces of Argentina and from other countries just to be a part of what God was doing. Pastors of all denominations showed up fifty or a hundred at a time and were changed. Most would fall in a heap under the power of God, and the Lord Himself would minister deeply to them.

Many of these leaders came from non-Pentecostal denominations, and when they reached their congregations, profound changes began taking place in the churches' worship, lifestyle, openness, and dependence on the Holy Spirit. What amazed us all so much was the willingness of so many pastors to seek God and show their hunger for His power by getting in their car or on a long-distance bus and traveling to where God was working in such an amazing way. Rey de Reyes Church had scores of people visiting them in every service from all over Argentina and from around the world for more than three years.

The same thing was happening during that intense time at Catedral de la Fe, the church Osvaldo Carníval pastors. At the beginning of this move in 1994, my wife, Sherry, our children, and I went to that church to see what God was doing. The emphasis during those wonderful days of amazement was the playfulness of God. The Lord was just sharing with us all His joy at being our Father, similar to the tone of Zephaniah 3:17, "He will joy over thee with singing." It was that night that our son got ministered to deeply by the power of God.

Humility

Behind the willingness to travel is the thought, "I need that moving in my own life. If I stay where I am and don't get in as close to it as possible, I may miss out on what God has for me." That eager searching, even though it may demand a very full evening or longer away from home, boils down to humility. I've heard people say, "God knows where I am so He can come and touch me when He gets around to it." But sometimes this can be a camouflage for arrogance. "He better bless me on my terms, because I'm not about to show the eagerness of a wide-eyed teenager over this." But why not? Jesus said that we have to become like a little child if we want to enter the kingdom of heaven. (See Matthew 18:3.)

Sergio Scataglini shares how he traveled to Argentina from the U. S. when he first heard that God was using his Bible school friend, Claudio Freidzon. "Claudio was a quiet, unassuming person," he thought. "How is it that God is using him so much? I've got to ask my old buddy and roommate to pray for me."

When he arrived at King of Kings Church and saw the

tremendous manifestations of God's power, he greeted his friend and thought Claudio would pray for him right away. But time went by past midnight and Claudio continued to pray for other people. "Doesn't he realize I've traveled a great distance to be here?" Sergio thought. Finally, at one o'clock, Claudio prayed for him and God's anointing and touch were very powerful. But it took humility to wait until last. It took a broken spirit to accept that his own friend give his time to ministering to others first. But the touch of God on Sergio's life has been so much the greater because he has learned to wait on God.

In one major region of Argentina a few years ago, many of the leaders showed a great deal of zeal to "protect the flock." However, in their earnest quality control they didn't take the time to check out what was happening. They prejudged the manifestations and the leaders God was using. Instead of wanting to see and learn about what was happening, they simply decided not to accept the revival. It didn't seem to fit into their grid. I'm glad that's not the way Paul and the church leaders were when it came to accepting the Gentiles.

In this particular region of Argentina not only did these leaders stay away from the many churches and areas where the Lord was working so powerfully, but they kept the people from becoming a part of what God was doing. That kept the region from experiencing His move for a few years.

A pastor's influence over his congregation and an overseer's control over his region is like a door. If the door opens wide, the whole church or the whole region can be blessed. If the door is firmly shut, God respects that choice made by one or a few that He has placed in authority. Some are so afraid of wildfire that when they see the neighbors out burning leaves, they invest all their energies in preparing their equipment just in case the fire gets out of hand. God help us to keep vigilant, but also to humbly get close to those bonfires and get in on the warmth and fellowship.

God and Man

What a delicate balance there is between God's grace and power and man's acceptance and participation. The right mix is crucial. The Holy Spirit is eager to work, if we will let Him. If we can receive what He has, there will always be more.

Let us not search after the signs or the manifestations or even the amazing fruit of revival. But let us seek God. When we give ourselves to Him, handing over all the personalized blueprints of preconceived ideas for how He is allowed to work, we will be invited into the river. Soon we won't be satisfied with wet ankles or wet knees. We will be swimming and totally abandoned to His care, to His creativity, and to His miraculous power.

8

Wonders, Gifts, and Miracles

OFTEN PEOPLE ASK us what we have we seen personally during this long-lasting move of God. If put alongside those accounts shared by first-hand eyewitnesses whom we trust, it would surely turn into a mountain. There's just so much to tell.

Sometimes folks want to know if we believe these things. Do we have a choice to disbelieve when we have been granted the joy and privilege of experiencing so much? Have we watched with a critical eye? Have we listened with an analytical perspective? Not anymore. The amount of raw data has overwhelmed us, and we have no reason to disbelieve the accounts. There are no hidden agendas of seeking gain from embellishing the story. Why do that when the truth is already so genuinely amazing that it could not have been invented by a cynic or a surreptitious salesman?

One of the favorite pastimes of Argentine Christians is to drink *mate* (an herbal tea) together and share testimonies of the miracles of God. I have traveled for hours by bus with pastors who have shared story after story without a pause. All of us have waited expectantly for that tiny break to chime in with one of our own.

The gifts of the Spirit are very much in operation here in Argentina. One sees them used constantly to build up and encourage the church. The Spirit is being poured out so there are dreams, visions, miracles, signs, and wonders.

In Acts 2:22 we see Peter preaching, saying that Jesus was "a Man attested by God to you by miracles, wonders, and signs" (NKJV). God verified the word that was spoken with His miracles, showing the message to be true.

At Centro Cristiano Nueva Vida, where Guillermo Prein is pastor, the GO (*grupos de oración*) or prayer cell group leaders are asked to record the miracles they see God perform. The number of miracles recorded over the last five years has averaged more than one thousand per year.

Pastor Alberto Scataglini has a team dedicated to intercession who records the mighty works of God. The list of miracles they have registered fills a large book of hundreds of pages.

The gifts of the Holy Spirit are accepted as everyday occurrences in the churches in Argentina. It is normal to hear someone say, "He gave me a word from God," or "My mother was healed of cancer, and that is why we are in the church today. Our whole family accepted Christ after that miracle."

SURPRISED BY THE SPIRIT

It was at the beginning of the wave of "the anointing" (*la unción*), and we had just finished a Missionary Fellowship meeting in which various members of the team commented on the signs and manifestations they had observed at Claudio Freidzon's church. Despite the skepticism expressed by some, God touched our group, and one of the ladies began laughing in the Spirit for quite a while. Amazement and consternation were the order of the day. That evening, various missionaries determined to go and see for themselves what was happening.

One of them was Rocco DiTrolio. Known for his perfectionism when he was in Bible college, no one at that time was surprised that he would be dusting his desk at one o'clock in the morning. He would turn the light off at his roommate's insistence, but in the dark one could still hear the furniture polish being sprayed to finish the desk cleaning.

When the ministers arrived at King of Kings Church, Rocco looked around at what was happening and was not very convinced at the sight. Suddenly the Holy Spirit touched his life, and in halting speech and strange tone he said, "I thought this was a show, but Jesus is here!" The witnesses on the day of Pentecost thought those Christians were drunk. Rocco might well have fit right in with the one hundred twenty. He fell to the ground, and his eyes closed.

"Help me carry him," said one of the missionaries.

"You brought him; you carry him out," he was told.

Almost two hours later, when they delivered him to his home, he still could not open his eyes. Ellen, his wife, was shocked and very worried at first, but soon he came around.

↓

Another missionary, Marc Triplett, attended a different service. Claudio Freidzon did not know Marc, but he picked him out of the crowd of hundreds of people and called him up to the platform. After falling once under the power of the Spirit, the norm is to have the ushers or workers carry the person off the platform. For some reason, Claudio kept Marc up on the platform and each of the twenty times that he tried to stand and walk off, the pastor would touch him again, and he would go down. During the next three months, each time Marc raised his hands, even to comb his hair, his knees would go weak, and he would almost fall under the power of God.

Later Marc and his wife, Jeannette, came to Buenos Aires with a busload of people from Bariloche, a tourist city two thousand kilometers south in the "Alps of Latin America" where they were starting a church. After the service, ten people had to be carried to the bus in a state of unconsciousness, the Spirit of God had touched them so much. Everyone else got off to have hamburgers at a fast-food restaurant, and these ten didn't even realize it. They were lost in the presence of God.

↓

A taxi driver was going past the church that Omar Olier pastors in Mar del Plata, a seaside city, when he found himself time after time circling the block where the church was. He could not quit driving past the church and around the block. Finally, he parked his vehicle and went into the church to find out what was happening. That was the night he gave his life to Jesus.

DREAMS AND VISIONS

"Your old men shall dream dreams, your young men shall see visions," the prophet foretold in Joel 2:28. I have heard quite a few tongue-in-cheek comments about the backward look of the aged men who are only left with dreaming dreams, but the context of the scriptures makes both dreams and visions future-directional. We don't really need the Holy Spirit to help us dream about what has happened. We certainly need His participation in projecting us toward His plans, a future of fruitfulness and sharing His glory.

So often the conversation with those who are not yet spiritually sensitive revolves either around the here and now or about projects that are attainable with a little personal dedication and hard work. The miraculous seems unnecessary. The surprising touch of God is not in those dreams.

Pastor Alberto Scataglini shared concerning a vision that Walter Llanos, a young man in his congregation had. Walter saw many people of the congregation walking up a hill, but they were on crutches and could only walk with great difficulty. When they reached the top of the hill, they would throw the crutches aside and begin to walk and run freely. The Lord laid the interpretation on Pastor Alberto's heart: Until that moment they were all leaning on human resources but a time was coming when they would depend totally on God, and He was about to do something very special among them.

A few days ago I asked the seniors at IBRP to do a little personal evaluation exercise with me that I learned from a graduate course in mentoring. On a sheet of paper I asked them all to draw a large circle. Inside the circle were to be those goals in life that have been attained. On the line the students were to write those goals that are not yet realized and outside the circle those that they have determined to release.

Let me quote some of the goals these revival dwelling students are committed to: "Preach the gospel to my biological father...Start a children's home...Start a business to support missionaries...Write a book...Create a praise chorus...Work with a choir of adolescents...Found and build transnational companies that can help open new churches and back pastors and missionaries...Preach the gospel around the world...Preach to stadiums full of people." They surely have some dreams and visions that the Lord has given them.

During these last few weeks God has given various young people at the school along with some visitors several visions that concur with one another. One young lady saw a whirlwind that began to spin and spin and reach out in power to the world. Another saw God's heart on the school begin to spin and spin until it reached out to the world. Another saw whirling fire going outwards. Firmly but tenderly God has been showing the students that they are a part of His activity that reaches out to touch the world.

Prophecy

Another demonstration of the outpouring of the Holy Spirit is, "Your sons and your daughters shall prophesy" (Joel 2:28). We rejoice in situations similar to those that occurred in Smith Wigglesworth's ministry such as announcing that the person standing on a rock in the back of the crowd was being healed of back problems. "Despise not prophecy" is a good rule to live by when the Holy Spirit is raising up young people who are called to prophetic ministries.

Hector Ferreyra has been on the cutting edge concerning prophetic words from the very beginning of his ministry. Before any of these amazing miracles and manifestations became part of our everyday lives, God spoke to him to take an alarm clock with him wherever he preached and declare: "The time is coming. God is going to do a mighty work. Many people will be saved." People considered him a little peculiar traveling around with his alarm clock, but God came through just as He had promised.

It was certainly a prophetic word God gave Carlos Annacondia: "Soon, soon, Argentina will be mine." None of us dreamed at the time that over one thousand one hundred people in one evening would surge forward to accept Christ "like thirsty cattle running toward water," as one observer stated.

I clearly remember a moment at the altar in the chapel at IBRP when an urgent prayer in tongues was understood and interpreted by Patricia Casas, a third-year student. The person was repeating: "If you don't go to the *pueblos* (small towns or people groups), who will go? If you don't go to the *pueblos*, who will go?"

Argentina as a nation at the end of 2001 experienced its worst political, economic and social crisis of the past seventy years. Two years before at the national pastors' conference, special speaker Edwin Alvarez brought this word: "Great changes are coming. Do not fear for what the nation must go through. There will be convulsions and movements. The political waters in Argentina will be agitated, but do not fear. When there are popular uprisings, when the economy of the nation teeters, do not fear . . . only remember that God already told you before it happens. God is preparing His church to go through any circumstance, political or economic, and to come out in victory. Raise your voice to confirm and to affirm your faith and to give confidence to the people. There will be figures that will fall, and there are men that today are in the heights that will be there no more. Let nothing harm or affect your heart."

In 1999 Argentina was considered an economic miracle and example. Who could have dreamed that two years later there would be economic collapse, popular demonstrations, road blockades, and various changes in government in two short weeks. But through this extremely difficult crisis starting in December of 2001 the church has opened soup kitchens and helped distribute welfare to thousands of people without jobs. God's church has ministered confidence to the people.

WORD OF KNOWLEDGE

Recently I heard of a minister who was speaking at a church in Lanús, a suburb of Buenos Aires. In the prayer line she came to a burly young man with a long ponytail who she sensed had been living a hardened lifestyle of sin, including drug and other addictions. The Lord showed her some things about him and tenderly she started saying, "You are thinking, 'How could God possibly forgive me? I have done so many bad things, and He would never accept me.' But the Lord wants you to know that He does accept you. He has died for you, and He loves you very much." As she continued in this vein, suddenly tears were coursing down the young man's cheeks. God promised that night to deliver him immediately from all his addictions that he had been struggling with for so long. There were more tears as the word of knowledge went forth. Then she said, "Receive the Spirit," reached up to touch him lightly on the forehead, and he went down in a heap under the Lord's power.

↓

Pastor and Prophet Oscar Ferreira had been invited to the Bible School to preach one night. He called asking directions, and the person who answered the phone at the guard's station happened to be a married student awaiting a call from her husband. As she gave him directions, he interrupted her with, "You have a burden to reach children in Africa."

At her initial response of amazement he stated, "Your husband is in prison and will get out when God says. Then you will minister to children in Africa." The call the student awaited was from the jail, and her husband was actually one of the inmates. They had fallen in love when she visited with the jail ministry team, and she had recently married him, despite the fact that he was still in jail.

That evening when Brother Ferreira started ministering in the chapel, he said, "I saw you today. Three of you were in your dormitory room wondering what you were doing here and whether God has anything for you next in ministry. Come up here to the altar if that describes you." Three recent graduates who had been working at the school as painters came forward, weeping from the depths of their hearts.

Then, he continued, pointing to another young woman in the audience. "I saw you today, standing with your cup, wondering if you really do have a call to reach children in another continent." Immediately this senior ran forward, crying out to God.

↓

I was leaving chapel after the morning service and noticed a young lady sitting alone in the middle of the sanctuary. I reached over to her and held her wrist briefly and said, "God sends you a hug." She began to sob. A few days later she shared with me that immediately before that moment she had been saying to the Lord, "I feel so lonely. If I could just receive a hug from you." That was when one of God's postmen arrived with a message for one of His daughters.

↓

God sometimes even shows us practical matters. Sherry and I were teaching in a couples' retreat in Cordoba, a city seven hundred kilometers from Buenos Aires. The campground chosen was rather rustic and included dirt paths between all the buildings. As I waited at the cafeteria table, my wife delayed longer and longer in arriving for supper. Finally, she walked in with a worried expression on her face. "I lost my contact lens," she said. At the time she was wearing rigid contact lenses, and it was her only pair.

I asked her where she had dropped it approximately, and she responded with an adamant, "Forget it! It is somewhere on a two block long dirt path." Despite her insistence that it was no use, I asked for a flashlight and went out praying that God would guide. The very first time I lowered the beam to look on the ground, I was pointing directly at the contact lens.

HEALINGS

A while ago we invited Pastor Horacio Baena to speak for an evening service at IBRP. He and his wife had been pastoring a small congregation faithfully for years after their graduation from the school. During ten years of pastorate, he had been asking the Lord for a healing ministry. He wondered if it was just a crazy idea or personal whim. Then he visited Catedral de la Fe where he was given a word of prophecy that God was answering his prayer. Suddenly God began to open doors of opportunity and to use him in the gift of healing. One campaign led to the other as God's power was shown.

The very evening that he was with us at River Plate Bible Institute, twenty-one different people were healed, most of them students. To celebrate the momentous event, we took a picture of all twenty-one with Pastor Baena. Many of the miracles had to do with curvature of the spine, back problems, and pain in the waist, which are so often related to having one limb shorter than the other. With no fanfare whatsoever, Horacio would sit the person on a chair, have them stretch their legs out in front of them and then quietly, he would say: "*Crece, crece, en el nombre de Jesús,*" or "Grow, grow, in the name of Jesus." Limbs would grow up to an inch in front of our eyes. A third-year student who had experienced pain in his waist and back for a number of years was healed that evening, and the pain disappeared for good. We placed the picture of the twenty-one people healed that night in our yearbook.

↓

Pastor Osvaldo Carníval shared recently about a lady who had come up to the platform at their church to give a testimony with her three-year-old daughter hanging on to her skirt. "My daughter had a brain tumor," the woman had said. "She had quit eating or moving around. As I was in the waiting room, expecting the worst, some ladies from the church shared God's Word with me and prayed." When the doctor came out to talk with her soon after that, she expected him to say, "She has passed away." Instead, he said, "She is beginning to respond and has asked for food." A week later the tests showed that the tumor had been absorbed and was gone. As the congregation clapped in jubilation, she continued, "Pastor, the testimony doesn't end there. The ladies had given me a Bible, and I opened it to Isaiah where it says that God gives us victory (*victoria* in Spanish). Right then I decided to go to the register of persons, and I changed my daughter's name to Victoria. God gave us victory!"

↓

Elena Díaz was teaching on the gifts of the Holy Spirit in a night Bible school. Feeling unqualified because of a lack of experience, this fourth-year student was trembling as she taught. Suddenly a student interrupted forcibly, "*¡Gloria a Dios por la hermana!* (Glory to God for the sister!)" He kept repeating it, to the puzzlement of Elena, and then they informed her that he had been mute until that class on healing. She kept trembling, but this time in awe of a wonderful God.

↓

I specifically remember one testimony from the King of Kings congregation. Lay people in the church had gone to pray for a boy in the children's hospital who had a tumor on his brain. The stench of the decomposing brain was evident in the hospital room. After these people of faith prayed, God performed a total healing.

↓

Evangelistic campaigns among Pentecostal churches include prayer for the sick. Some of the healings that take place include healing from paralysis, the closing up of open wounds that have not healed properly for months and the healing of many ailments like astigmatism. One of the healings that is truly creative is when a lady is told to hold on to her skirt because God is going to be taking her excess weight. The women who have disbelieved were thankful that they wore a slip that day because suddenly they have found that their skirts have fallen around their ankles due to the tremendous and instantaneous loss of weight.

In a recent campaign with Fernando Nielsen, a Baptist pastor from Bridge of Life Church, Alberto Romay reports that teeth filled miraculously; five or six with gold and the others with an unknown material. The dentists were amazed.

Cancer of the bones and of the lungs disappeared in the town of San Fernando. One lady had breast cancer. She went to the bathroom to check and even the rough skin over the tumor had scarred instantly. People also left their walking sticks and their wheelchairs because their curvature of the spine was healed. Addictions were also healed.

This evangelist is often used in the healing of flat feet, and I have watched as arches formed in the feet of a youth pastor from Florida. He no longer needed the plastic inserts in his shoes. Another time one of the women on a visiting team from

Minnesota also had her feet healed. When they covered her feet in oil, and she stood on paper, it was evident that she now had arches. She shared that she had severely turned in feet when she was a baby and had undergone several operations on her feet as a child. She was now in college track, and her problems had caused severe pain as she ran. Tears streamed down her face as she realized that the Lord had touched her.

↓

Our evangelism students often take the Bible school's van to various places, but this day it happened to be to Ramallo, a town in the interior. They shared the gospel through drama, mime, and testimonies. As one of our seniors was walking down the street, he noticed a family who had taken their ten-year-old son, a boy totally paralyzed, out to lie in the sun.

Suddenly the student sensed the Holy Spirit saying, "Hug him." Another voice insinuated how ridiculous he would feel doing it, but he firmly decided to obey God. When he held the boy, the lifeless body felt like jelly, but the youngster got his hug anyway. Just recently we received word that the child is entirely healed.

INNER HEALING

One evangelist said, "When people who are in anguish or depressed come to the campaign, many times by the discernment that God gives us, we can see that they have even tried to commit suicide. In that moment we declare the word that God gives us, and the people are set free. That impacts us because we see the deep changes as the Spirit begins to flow."

So often people have many hurts that have made inner wounds. Though they have tried to get over these things, sometimes the pain is so deep that there is still an ache. As the Lord begins to minister to them, one can watch the person being touched by the Spirit who helps them let go of their past pain, often through weeping. Sometimes this is followed by a time of releasing laughter and joy that comes upon the person.

Other times the Lord's Spirit overwhelms people, and they fall under the power of God. In this time as the individual is in the presence of God, He shows them something that brings a release or healing. It is almost as if while under anesthetic, the person's hurts are operated on by a Master surgeon. The Spirit is ever so careful to use just the right instrument and tenderly remove the thing that hurts.

One of our students gave testimony to the fact that her mother had suffered from depression for ten years and that someone invited her to church, where God healed her totally. Another shared that she had personally gone into such a depression that she would not leave her room for six months. Then someone arrived at her house with the Good News.

Someone I knew once ministered to one of our students, having a vision of their hurting heart. It was marred, stoney, and hardened from some difficult experiences in the past, but the vision continued as the Lord's hand took that heart and proceeded to soften it and then to decorate it tenderly as a valentine with lace, bows, and beauty. The student wept in the Lord's presence and experienced a release, and God brought a healing.

Deliverance From Demonic Possession

"This Easter weekend we got to see dozens who were freed of demonic possession, and at least two hundred people accepted the Lord," testified an IBRP student. In Argentina, this is not an unusual testimony. Seeing people get set free from the power of the enemy is a normal event.

↓

La Iglesia el Buen Pastor of Lomas de Zamora, where José Vena is pastor, evangelizes by sending teams of three out door-to-door to ask to pray for people's needs.

A gruff "I'm of another religion" is answered by, "Why don't you pray according to your religion, and then we will pray."

"You go ahead and pray," they usually say. "I don't know how." Every week people are visited until there is a decision, and then they are invited to a home group in their neighborhood. If the family is not open at all, the address is written down and sent to the intercessors for prayer.

A prayer team encountered a home where they were taken to a back room and found there a teenaged girl who looked disheveled and wild. No one in the neighborhood even knew of her existence. The believers prayed in the name of Jesus and this person who was bound for years was set free. She now sits in church, clothed and in her right mind, just like the Gadarene demoniac. (See Mark 5:1–20.)

↓

An IBRP evangelism team shared about their recent ministry. One of the seniors asked Martin, a freshman, to pray for people. As he would begin to pray, people would fall down under the power of God. A woman had gone forward who mentioned back problems, curvature of the spine, and pain throughout her body. As Martin prayed, the lady started groaning as her vertebrae cracked one after the other. She was both healed and delivered of demonic power at the same time. That is an interesting outreach outing for a freshman student!

↓

Corina, one of our students, had been mentored as a witch by her mother and grandmother. Her family was involved in the occult for years, and she had become bound by demons. The artists and politicians would come to her house to get their fortune told.

"I had contact with this from the time I was very young," Corina said. "I spent months at my grandmother's house, and

I was like her disciple. As I grew up it was a normal life for me to practice witchcraft and read cards. At twenty years old, when I accepted the Lord and left all of this, my family kicked me out of the house. It produced a spiritual clash in me."

"Her blood pressure would go down; she would faint or manifest, speaking with a man's voice," explained her husband, Marcelo. "After she became a Christian, we prayed for her for eight or nine days."

"The spiritual world was not new to me," Corina explained. "I had knowledge of spiritual practices, and Marcelo tells of how I would become transformed and levitate. This was normal for me. To see demons and to be involved in the spiritual world was not something unusual."

Corina, however, experienced something different spiritually when she became a Christian. "For the first time in my life I began to feel a freedom and a peace. Hatred was part of our life in my family, and now I found myself loving even those who had rejected me. That seething hatred was gone from me."

↓

Carlos Annacondia and his evangelistic team offer a very creative ministry to individual churches. During a month his team preaches at the church helping everyone develop their faith and a level of expectation concerning the evangelistic event. They also prepare the workers of the church to counsel those who will be accepting Christ and to minister deliverance. Evangelist Annacondia preaches one night, but the groundwork has been laid for God to work mightily, and a team has been permanently trained.

When the team was at Avance Cristiano church in Temperley, where Edgardo Muñoz is pastor, one of the workers they prepared for deliverance ministry was our son, Nathan. The night Brother Carlos preached, we had four hundred visitors. This was a 40 percent increase in our normal church attendance. When the altar call came to accept Christ, they all moved forward en masse. Ten people manifested demons, so they were carried to one of the classrooms. Nathan had the opportunity to pray with one man, and he did as he had been taught, asking him if he harbored bitterness toward anybody. "Yes," was his answer, "toward my father who abused me sexually during ten years." When people are desperate they tend to face the real issues. As Nathan prayed, the man was totally set free.

For years every church had an intercession ministry team that prayed during the services as well as a deliverance ministry team. I have seen the church kitchen used as a deliverance room or even a little tent out behind the church. Deliverance is a normal part of our lives.

Signs and Wonders

Signs and wonders have become the norm among us. In June of 2003, an evangelism team of young people from the United States had just arrived at the Bible school after being on an all-night flight. As they were eating lunch before going to rest after a ten-hour flight, I noticed that a visiting evangelist was chatting with a pastor from the Congregational church. Since we often invite people to share testimonies when a team is here, I asked Alberto to tell about the campaigns he had been in recently.

After less than ten minutes of translated testimony he started to pray for those on the team who were sick. Among the needs that God touched that day was a young man who had a herniated disc. God healed him instantly. The evangelist asked him to pick up another young man, and he did so and carried him for one hundred feet. Then he went out to run, activities that would have made him groan in agony just minutes before.

Why do we see miracles today? So much of the reason behind these amazing manifestations of God's power is the love of God drawing sinners to Himself. Even one or two healings can open up an entire community so that the Word of salvation can be preached. It is evident that the Lord's willingness to heal is in direct proportion to His willingness to impact the lives of sinners.

The purpose of signs and wonders is to confirm the bold speaking forth of the Word. Part of the authority He gives us is to make disciples and bring them into wholeness.

God's Amazing Provision

Among the many acts of God that we see here are those regarding God's provision. How vividly I remember a conversation with Damián González when he was still a student at IBRP. Bible school is rarely a time of superfluity, and Damián was among those who had to trust God for each month's school bill payment. He shared concerning a detailed list of needs and wants he had written up and began praying about. It included a new suit, three dress shirts, a briefcase, a belt, a wallet, and some other items.

A few days after bringing this list before the Lord, he received a call from a lady who had heard his testimony and preaching on the radio. "My husband recently passed away," she stated. "He so appreciated your message and your testimony. Would you mind if I gave you some of the almost new items from his wardrobe?" Being a very bright Bible school student, Damián did not pass up this evident divine appointment. The lady sent him two new suits, various classy dress shirts, a new briefcase, two belts, and a new wallet. God was building his faith and trust, and hearing about it helped the rest of us too.

↓

Sherry, my wife, was in a ladies' convention in Mar del Plata when a woman shared that she had brought only forty pesos for food for the three days. God asked her to put all of it in the offering. She obeyed and at last count kept finding more money in her purse—upwards of sixty pesos, and the provision still had not run out!

↓

One young man shared in chapel about his desire to eat some candy. He had absolutely no money. Suddenly a bus raced past him and a ten-peso bill floated out of the door! Candy money and more.

Another one of our students was always giving away any money he received, buying needed supplies like shampoo for his friends and not keeping anything for himself. He had recently given away his black shoes. A visitor came to the Bible school and felt led by the Lord to buy this young man a black suit. The student didn't have one, but the visitor (not knowing the full story) also threw in two new dress shirts and ties, a dress belt, and black shoes.

↓

We have lived through so many economic crises here in Argentina during the last few years. There were times that inflation hit a percentage and a half a day. Many years, when we wanted to remember the price of bread or milk one year before, we would just take a zero off the present price. In the midst of some of those deep crises, families often had to take turns to go to church because they couldn't afford bus money for everyone to make it at the same time.

It was during one of those very critical moments that Pastor-evangelist Fernando Junco was invited to minister in a church in a very poor neighborhood. Silvia, his wife, grew pale as she listened to her husband saying, "On your way home tonight and during the day tomorrow, keep your eyes open as you walk. God has told me that he is sending angels to place cash bills in the gutters for you to find." During the next couple of days, many of those desperately poor church members found up to two hundred pesos at a time lying on the street.

GUIDANCE

In the year of 1999 in southern France, a young pastor's daughter was sharing with her friends concerning her feeling that she needed to train for the ministry in Argentina. It seemed totally ridiculous to her and to her parents. Suddenly, as she spoke, a five-cent coin from Argentina hit the wooden floor of her bedroom. Amazed at God's evident confirmation, her parents accepted that she travel to another continent for her ministerial training. In a service recently, Marie Eve Gonzalez shared that she still had that little coin in her jewelry box.

↓

When Alejandro Savenko was six years old, he was thrown in the river by his neighbors just because he was an evangelical believer. A year later, when he was seven, it happened again, but this time the swirling waters were taking him to the bottom. His lungs had been deprived of oxygen for quite a while when God miraculously helped him to walk out onto the shore. Those times behind the iron curtain were dangerous for the Ukranian Christians. The church he attended had no men. They had been taken out and shot for their faith. Most of the Bibles in use were versions that had been copied into notebooks partly to avoid detection by the secret police. During his time of military service he was beaten repeatedly for his unwillingness to sing certain violent war songs. Due to the many beatings, his kidneys dropped three inches, causing him constant pain.

After his release from military service, Alejandro had worked hard to buy a piece of land and had purchased all of the materials to build a house when God led him to sell it all and "Go to Argentina." His mother was aghast and attempted to dissuade him. In a flash of insight he presented the following proposition. "If you take the responsibility for my dis-obeying what God wants me to do, I will gladly stay here." His mother relented and decided to pray a blessing over him before his trip.

Without so much as an address in his pocket he set sail for Buenos Aires. He wondered where he would go in Argentina and what he would do to make a living. Alejandro didn't know a word of Spanish, but God intervened. Within half an hour after he walked off the ship, he was led to a Ukranian pastor who in turn sent him to the home of some Ukranian believers from his church. As the pastor presented him to the lady of the house, she asked if sharing with their children would bother him. "Not at all," he answered, amazed at their open hospitality.

"What is your name?" the church member asked.

"Alejandro Savenko," he answered.

"Of the Savenkos from Zhitomir?" she asked. When he confirmed the location of his hometown, she was astonished. The Holy Spirit spoke to his heart: "She lived in your home for three years when you were a baby." From the time of his birth until he was three years old, Alejandro's parents had offered open and generous hospitality to the lady. Originally unaware of his identity, she and her husband now were doing the same for him in the foreign land of Argentina nineteen years later.

They put him in touch with Pastor Carlos Kucharenko of Paraná, Entre Ríos in the northeastern portion of Argen-tina. When they met, Pastor Carlos informed him that he had been invited to preach in the Ukraine and that he needed a translator. "But I don't know Spanish," Alejandro objected.

"You have three months to prepare," he was informed by the pastor. God worked another miracle, and he was able to learn the language and take high school equivalency tests in Spanish during those three months. The trip to the Ukraine was a great blessing and upon their return Pastor Kucharenko put him in touch with IBRP. He is a recent graduate who went back to the Ukraine. God told him to quit his job there, and a week later he received a call from Pastor-evangelist Hector Ferreyra asking him to coordinate his campaigns in that country. A few months later, up to nine thousand were hearing the gospel, and many healings were taking place. In a three-day event, four hundred fifty people accepted Christ. Alejandro's present project is coordinating a campaign with Evangelist Carlos Annacondia. The Lord certainly does guide our paths.

↓

As I was grading papers in my office one day, missionary-teacher Cynthia Nicholson walked in with a harried look on her face. "What's the matter?" I queried.

"I forgot my purse on the bus," she responded with a very worried look. Replacing documents is not an easy matter, so we both realized the import of the situation.

"Let's pray," I said, and we did, right then. She went on to teach her music class, and I continued grading papers for about forty-five minutes. Suddenly I sensed that it would be good to stop one of the buses from that line to get the word out that she had left her purse.

As I waited on one side of the street, a bus of that line was coming from the other direction. I crossed and flagged the driver down. "A friend of mine left a purse on one of your buses . . ." I began to say.

"What does she look like?" asked the driver. As I described the blonde lady who had ridden the bus, he picked up an item sitting next to him. "Is this it?" he said, showing me the purse. Everything was intact, and God's timing of every detail was perfect.

↓

Claudio Freidzon shares how he first met his wife, Betty. They were both teenagers and had gone to a youth camp that was held at IBRP. One afternoon he heard a beautiful choir practicing in the chapel and went to check it out. A sixteen-year-old young lady was directing the choir, and as he watched her, he not only was smitten with her beauty but also with her demeanor. Too shy to approach her, he just watched from a distance and found out that her name was Betty and that she lived on Bucarelli Street.

As the days went by, he could not get her out of his mind. So he went and asked his pastor what to do. "Go find her and ask her dad if you can be her friend" was his answer. But knowing only the street name in a city of millions, it was going to be next to impossible. Claudio began to walk up and down that street which is over one hundred twenty-seven blocks long. He would ask in each of the blocks if they knew a young lady in the neighborhood whose name was Betty. He felt rather foolish, until he asked a lady in a certain neighborhood who answered that maybe it was the grocer's daughter. When Claudio asked the owner of the grocery store if he knew of a Betty who was an evangelical Christian, his future father-in-law replied, "She is my daughter."

Recently I asked the Dean of IBRP, Ernesto Nanni, to tell me once again about an experience that he often mentions when teaching on the Book of Acts. In his own words:

> Claudio Freidzon had asked me to have some informal teaching times with the volunteer workers of his church. It was at the beginning of the move of God we call the anointing. Every Tuesday I would go to teach and spend time with the hundreds of workers.
>
> One day I was about to start the class when Claudio appeared. Since we were about to pray, I invited him to pray for the beginning of class.
>
> "Are you sure that you want me to pray?" he asked. This was because so many explosive things were happening at that time. I assented.
>
> He prayed for all the leaders, and I observed how they received, along with diverse manifestations. They wept; they laughed; others would fall down.

When he finished praying for everyone else he prayed for me. That was when I experimented with something special and new for me. I fell to the floor, and was there at least thirty minutes under the anointing. I felt a special joy and a new anointing—something different. I then attempted to start the class but could not. I kept trying but was having different sensations. I would laugh, I would cry...At first I thought it was just one more experience but was not aware of the long-range effect of that experience.

That same week I was giving classes about the Holy Spirit at the church of Pastor Adrián Juniors. It was the last of four classes. My first three classes had been very systematic, very theological, and very deep. I always say that the Holy Spirit had not even passed near that class. That last week when I started to give the class, the Spirit fell on us all, and more than 200 people received the baptism of the Holy Spirit. I was amazed at myself. That was not habitual in my ministry.

Later I meditated on this and realized that I had received something special that Tuesday and that never again would I judge external manifestations of the Holy Spirit because I could never know what He was doing internally.[1]

Wrap-Up

How good it is to be in a place where God is constantly at work! We know that He is alive, and therefore He is active. His body, the church, is open to working in the gifts of the Spirit. They know they are serving a mighty God for whom nothing is impossible. This belief and faith allows the Lord to show Himself strong in a multitude of situations.

The programs and systems for the church are not sufficient. We need the power of the Holy Spirit flowing through them! As Pastor Carnival once said, "It is not enough to have the words alone or the music alone. We need both in order to have the song." This song is the working of God among His people, who in turn can sing to a dying world: He IS alive!

Since this is so, we need to realize that we can live in continuous revival. A God who is alive and active expects us to be the same.

9

Living in Continuous Revival

GOD'S POWER IS still being seen in this blessed land. We recently had several students whose curvatures of the spine were healed at a service. Just today I heard the testimony of a fourteen-year-old who happened to be visiting his family on campus and was healed. "I have brand new feet!" he said with amazement.

One pastor whose eyes had become dry because of a malfunction of his tear ducts began to weep in a pastors' school devotional and later shared in class, with tears of gratitude, "I have had to walk around with a little bottle to help lubricate my eyes. For the first time in eight years I have tears!"

A month ago Dr. Carolyn Tennant preached at our church, Avance Cristiano. During the altar time the Holy Spirit descended on the congregation, and so many were weeping. As the musicians took their places at the end of the service, they sat in silence and also wept. The pastors' sons, Fernando and Leandro Muñoz, were at the saxophone and keyboard. One of the other musicians looked at them and saw fire coming from them and enveloping him. He also stopped playing, and we all sat in silence for a long time in God's presence.

Three days later a lady from the church was sharing with one of the leaders, "On Sunday I saw fire surrounding the musicians." There had been no contact between these firsthand witnesses of the continuing fresh fire of God for the next generation.

Another woman in our church testified that during a prayer meeting several weeks before, she had been exhorted to pray for the nations rather than herself. "When we think about others instead of ourselves, we often receive what we need," the prayer leader had told everyone. The woman had been having much pain in her stomach area and other problems over a five-year period. During the prayer time she was healed, and she discharged numerous large and small kidney stones then and in the next several days, with the pain entirely going away after all those months.

A student once told of her experience when a special speaker in an evening service singled her out from the crowd and stated that God was taking away the pain from her heart. "I felt like someone had reached in and extracted a big piece of darkness out of my heart, and now I keep looking at it, and it is a heart filled with light."

Twenty years have passed since that first powerful campaign with Carlos Annacondia in La Plata. We recently invited him to speak in our chapel service at IBRP, and the passion is still as strong and as fresh as ever.

Lately, we have been experiencing prophetic words, healings, the electrifying power and presence of God, baptisms in the Holy Spirit, young people at the altars weeping for an hour as they accept the call, people getting saved as our students go downtown to evangelize, and a service that lasted five hours.

Claudio Freidzon had thought the move of God would be for a season and asked the Lord how long it would continue. The answer God gave him was that it would be with us as long as we were willing to seek Him. In other words, it is an open-ended commitment on God's part, contingent on our availability.

How do we live personally and corporately in a continuing revival? Once again, there is no formula, but there do exist principles, which will augment the freedom for the Holy Spirit to continue to work.

We began to learn that there are certain things we must do to stay in revival. There are also certain things we must avoid. The Holy Spirit can get grieved and leave. It is easy to fall into certain pitfalls through our own human desires and flesh. The dangers are always lurking, and it behooves us to be warned about them.

Pride

One of the dangers in a time of revival is pride. The leader gets accustomed to the working of the supernatural, loses his awe at being used of God, and ultimately fails to depend on God. The gifts of the Holy Spirit continue to work through the person's life, but in the end God has to find someone else to carry forward the revival.

This happened with one young man who in his time of training would walk on an elevator and the demon-possessed would fall writhing on the elevator floor. In one three-week campaign in the interior of the country this young man saw 1,300 people accept Christ. But the power went to his head. Instead of being at people's disposition, his attitude was, "Let them find what they can at the campaign." For years, God's power lifted from him.

Another young minister who was mightily used of God stated once, "The Holy Spirit is like a motorcycle. You just get on and ride." God took him to an early reward.

Ministers who judged, compared themselves with and harshly criticized those whom God was using are no longer with us on this earth. The holiness and power of God must leave us in awe. The glory has to be Christ's and His alone!

PROTECTIONISM

The attitude of protectionism is similar to the spirit of Ananias and Sapphira. (See Acts 5:1–11.) It goes something like this: "We can't trust God with everything. It is too much for Him to handle. We'll take care of a portion and reserve it for ourselves. We will make our own decisions about it."

Many pastors have had this attitude when it comes to committing the totality of their own personal lives or turning their congregations wholly over to God. "What if people see something unusual and don't come back?" is a question that spells death.

It is not our responsibility to "protect" people from what God Himself wants to do in their lives. He must have complete control of everything.

A SPIRIT OF COMPETITION

Another marked danger is a spirit of competition. With the tremendous proliferation of cell groups here, numbers can become a motivator and a source of pride. How many cell groups do you have? How large is your cell group? How many people are you baptizing each time? These are fine questions to ask as long as we are still truly caring about people.

Once I asked Evangelist Carlos Annacondia how many people had accepted the Lord through his ministry. "I quit counting," he answered. "So many different people participate in a person's coming to Christ. What I do know is that about five hundred thousand raised their hands and filled in decision cards in a one-year period. But after that I quit counting. Actually, God told me to quit counting. He asked me what purpose I had in doing that." Although there is a book in the Bible called Numbers, God undoubtedly is pleased with this humble spirit.

CORRUPTION

One of the aspects of life and religion that brought the wrath of God on the Canaanites was worshiping Baal, but in the form of worshiping their own king. Whatever he said could not be questioned since he was a god.

Unscrupulous leaders can bandy about the phrase "touch not my anointed," but for their own self-aggrandizement. God will not continue to allow His river to flow if the leadership of the church is taken up in seeking position and wealth. Even if it is subtly covered up, God knows.

SPIRITUAL BOREDOM

Isaiah 43:22 says, "But you have not called upon Me, O Jacob; And you have been weary of Me" (NKJV). Another danger to continuing in revival is weariness. Making evangelism, worship, and discipleship the center of your life for long hours every day can begin to wear down the leadership if there isn't a continuing, personal renewal in the swirling pools and eddies of God's river.

One of our leaders once said he was tired of hearing about miracles. That certainly is the threshold of burnout. What could be more exciting than hearing about God's power made manifest? A healing evangelist mentions that there are few who weep in brokenness and gratitude when God graciously hands them a healing. They have lost the awe. It can become an attitude of spiritual entitlement. If we are not careful, we can become accustomed to the powerful acts of our divine King.

DISTRACTION

Losing focus is another critical danger area concerning revival. If we do not love people into the kingdom, revival is not for us. But many churches determined to hold their own conference or run to the next international conference. Some of this was undoubtedly of God, but these things can also be mere distractions, fluff that scatters our thinking and our spirits.

Many leaders believe that the revival must permeate all of society, including politics. They dream of the country having a born-again president in a rather naive, "kingdom now" mentality. The idea is that if we can just get the *caudillo* (strongman) in our camp, the nation will be saved. Some pastors have even run for political office and, thankfully, have lost at the polls.

"I send you forth as lambs among wolves" (Luke 10:3). This does not bespeak a strong political presence by the church. Neither does "wise as serpents, and harmless as doves" (Matt. 10:16). We should not become a part of the world's power mongering.

INFLEXIBLE STRUCTURES

Though the individual church cell-based structure is critical to much of the multiplication and growth we are seeing, it cannot cancel out the opportunity to bring the entire congregation together for an evangelistic campaign or to cooperate with various groups in that type of effort. Unfortunately, some of our churches are beginning to look like islands because the structure does not allow for cooperative efforts between churches.

There is no structure that can take the place of trusting God. The Lord likes organization and order. This is apparent when one sees our organized world, but the structure can't take the place of the life of the Spirit. One still has to stay open to the new things God wants to do and to allow the Spirit of God to lead.

"Many people who visit here," said Pastor Guillermo Prein, "want to know what I do to get this kind of growth. They want the methods and the system handed to them. They ask for the paper and the program, but there is no shortcut to meeting God."

In the United States we tend to go for method. We read; we

buy materials; we try out what someone else has done success-fully. "We might as well," we say. "Why reinvent the wheel?"

However, we may be circumventing the very thing God wants from us most: to seek His face. There is no substitute for this. God wants us to turn to Him for everything. We have to pray. We must spend time in His presence. These are what our churches need most, and no methods or systems, ideas or programs will ever satisfy. Guillermo Prein ended with another comment, "It is not just an easy method. It cost my whole life, you know."

Majoring on the Spectacular and Abandoning Apostolic Practice

T. J. Jones, a teacher at North Central University, used to say, "I don't care how high you jump, as long as you walk straight when you come back down." Openness to the Holy Spirit and the necessary flexibility to allow Him to do His work are not synonymous with forgetting our roots. We still must disciple and baptize new believers. We must teach them about stewardship and pray with them to receive the baptism in the Holy Spirit.

I recently heard Carlos Annacondia say that the power and the transformation are not in falling down or laughing or shaking, which are all fine. "The power comes with the baptism of the Holy Spirit accompanied by speaking in tongues, and we must continue to emphasize it," he urged strongly.

Though corporate worship is awesome and overwhelming, we must not lose sight of the individual's baptism in the Holy Spirit with power. God's presence is so evident in diverse manifestations, but we must continue to emphasize and teach that each one needs to "tarry...until you are endued with power from on high" (Luke 24:49, NKJV).

Hardness Instead of Softness

Those who have studied the history of revivals know that there is always a backlash during a move of God. Resistance, criticism, rumors, gossip, even insults are part and parcel of seeking the glory of God. Some people get hard.

The natural man, entrenched and comfortable, often feels judged and disparaged when someone shows up and says that God is doing miracles. "Why can't I be used like that?" they wonder. They begin to ridicule the work rather than to face these feelings of inadequacy. So often the reason leaders stay away from revival meetings is that they don't want their constituency to think they value what is happening, or because they don't feel they are able to "duplicate" these things for the people. Although man cannot duplicate things, God will do even more if we are willing to risk, to move outside our comfort zone when He calls us to it.

We have to be soft and not rigid. We must be willing to let the new wine of the Holy Spirit bubble and have His way. Dry and rigid wineskins cannot hold the new wine. They will crack and break, letting the wine spill out, and both will be lost. (See Matthew 9:17.)

We must be open to what God has for us. Desirous of all He wants, we cannot let ourselves get hardened in our old traditions or stiffen against His new plans. In order to let the new wine in, there has to be a continuing desire for it. We must have faith that He will act, along with a sense of expectancy and preparation so that we are ready when He moves. We have to believe that God will use even us.

Not in Tune for Worship

The Person of Christ is pre-eminent. It is important to lift Him up with the emphasis on His Person. It is not the professional quality of the worship team or the way they are dressed. If worship gets perfunctory, we are in trouble. If it becomes a show, that is grievous. Worship is not entertainment. We are not there to see how good the band is or how well someone can sing. It is not to judge the sound system or to be distracted by choreography.

How often we see tears streaming down people's cheeks during worship. Those are real, and they are from the heart. God delights in genuine expressions of commitment and love, and He honors us with His presence. When it gets tinny, the Holy Spirit will not be in evidence.

The worship team should be more concerned about the spiritual aspects of worship than they are about anything else. The group can be well-practiced, the sound checks made, and everybody can look good, but if the worship team is not in tune with God, then it hinders the work He wishes to do.

In 2 Chronicles 20:20–25 we see that the choir, of all things, was sent to go before the soldiers into battle. In actuality, they were the true warriors. Scripture tells us that as this choir began to sing and praise the Lord, He set up ambushes among the enemy troops and they killed each other off. Spiritual warfare is accomplished by the worship team. They can defeat the enemy with true praise and prepare the way for God to move in the delivery of the prophetic word. Opening is given for deliverance, healing, and other miracles. How critical that the musicians be prayed up, spiritually astute, and prepared to lead the people into true worship.

NEGLECTING TIME WITH GOD

Revival living takes time. Seeking God above all else is an activity that does not mesh too well with an agenda so packed and structured that there is no time to meditate, intercede, or even to banter with the bank teller or checkout person at the grocery store. Many of us get frustrated if we miss the first section of a revolving door we want to enter. Our lives are so pressured by the wrong kingdom that we cannot see that the kingdom is among us.

Paying attention to God and giving Him our time is crucial. After all, if the president of our country entered our room, we would surely stop and pay attention to him. How much more so when it comes to God?

I remember one moment in the nineties when God's Spirit began a sovereign work on campus. At that time hardly anyone fell under the power of God. One day in class the students started falling out of their desks. No one knew what was happening, but we understood it was holy. One wise teacher allowed the students to stay on the floor and prayed with the whole class for a time. Another quickly pressed for the students to be lifted off the floor so he could start the class. That was the year that eight of our students got "stuck" in tongues. For days they could not speak Spanish.

One girl kept an accent that sounded like she was from Central America for months. She would get on the bus in her hometown and say a couple of words and the bus driver would ask, "Where are you from?"

Her answer, "From right here, San Nicolás."

"Why do you talk like that?" he would ask inquisitively.

"It is a sign from God that He loves this community." Often that would mean open doors to share testimony and the gospel. Had we not taken some time in the schedule for prayer, we would have missed all that God had for us.

Each Christian should know what it is like to be lost in God's presence. Going beyond the ankle-deep water to the knee-deep takes a purposeful wading out. If you are going to get out in the deep where you will be able to abandon yourself on the water's buoyancy and swim, it will take time.

How often we drive past that little brook with the inviting, cold water that would so refresh us if we just "went wading." But I have promises to keep, and expectations must be met. The thought, *What will they say if* . . . keeps us away from that beautiful river. We must hurry on. No time to take off our shoes and socks. How surprised we would be to see that brook changed later on its way so that it became deep enough to swim in and thereby be transformed. Wading out into the deep means purposeful movement into the current.

If you are going to be moved emotionally, it takes time. If you are going to meditate deeply, it takes time. If you are going to bask in God's presence and receive visions and dreams from Him, it takes time. If you refuse to take the time, none of these things can happen.

We have learned to allow a little margin in the schedule at IBRP. Sometimes it has to be more than a little. Our all-school prayer service happens every other Thursday evening, alternating with full services. The prayer meeting starts at nine thirty, just after suppertime here, and we normally pray for about an hour. Tonight past midnight the students were still praying. Many had been renewed in the Spirit or received specific words from Him. When there is a scheduled time that we all meet together for prayer, the opportunity is much more viable for the Lord to work. Then we like to give that extra space and time as God is moving.

We hold a day of fasting and prayer together every quarter. God has done such amazing things in the students' lives on those days when we regularly take time apart to seek Him together. Ho-hum predictability with no special times to seek Him end up flat boring.

At three of the major churches here in Buenos Aires, they schedule a week or two per year that are called "Weeks of Consecration." These are impacting moments in God's presence when people take time, with no rush, for the Lord to show them where changes should be made. This means God leads the churches into fresh things. He touches them, renews them, keeps them in continual revival.

Not Making Revival a Singular Event

Some revivals have lasted for only a short time because the leadership cancelled everything very abruptly, and the revival became a paramount event that swallowed up life. There were people here in Buenos Aires who lost their jobs because they just didn't make it to work after being in service after service. Revival like this cannot be sustained. It simply becomes a bittersweet memory and is no more.

At IBRP we have attempted to stretch the structures to give place to a move of God, but in such a way that revival can be part of our lives. It accompanies us instead of cancelling out our regular lives. In this way we can live in the flow for years.

When we act like God is moving among us is a major exception, we tend to relegate it to history. When we allow Him to teach us about stretchy wineskins, then He can work time and again and surprise us on an ongoing basis.

Our relationship with God is often compared in the Word with the marriage relationship. He is the Bridegroom; the church is the bride. (See Revelation 19:7; Isaiah 54:5.) Sherry and I sometimes notice couples in a café, sitting there, saying nothing. He is involved with the newspaper, and she is lost in the oblivion of her husband's neglect. They are married, but there is no connection, no romance, and no sparkle in their eyes. It is the same if the Christian simply relies on his contract deed of salvation, but does not enjoy being in God's presence. They have to develop an ongoing relationship, keep talking, and maintain surprises and romance.

Likewise, it is very difficult to live a constant honeymoon for more than a few days, and it would tend to get boring. When romance is everything, it loses its magic. When it is a part of everything intermittently, it charms constantly, renews as needed, refreshes, and surprises.

If a few manifestations would have made us cancel all classes for two weeks, we would have had a few of those times in the last twenty years and no more. But with a regular prayer time together, individual prayer in the early mornings and evenings, a day of fasting and prayer every quarter, services that major on altar times every two weeks, and chapel services that can go long yet not 'X' out the classes of that day, we tend to live in the brightness of the fire of Pentecost on an ongoing basis. God is constantly talking to us, surprising us with miracles, and showing us His love. It is this way with the churches, as much as with the Bible school. That is why revival has been alive for so many years here in Argentina.

A Lack of Holiness

True revival affects our conversation, our thought life, the jokes we tell, our kidding, our reactions, and our TV watching.

Carlos Annacondia long ago got rid of television. He knows that it affects him and stays away. This is not a new legalism or a pantywaist approach to temptation. This is practical and real tenacity in order to stay close to God.

A phrase often quoted from Claudio Freidzon by his close friends is, "The little dove will fly away" (if you say that or do this). Grieving the Spirit should be a major object of study and meditation for us if we are interested in living a continuing revival.

Neglecting Fasting

We are not meant to neglect the discipline of fasting. It needs to keep coming up for us. We can't look back at a time we once did it and be satisfied with the past.

Today I spoke with Ricardo Cacabelos, a pastor who worked with Steve Hill in a church plant years ago. He and his wife were new Christians but became pastors of this work while they were still in Bible school. He has nine workers at IBRP at present and is a strong backer of missions.

In the conversation, I was recommending that he take some continuing education with Latin American Advanced School of Theology. "I don't think so right now," he answered very naturally and nonchalantly, with not an iota of self-congratulation. "Since 1999 I have given myself to fasting. In the last four years I have fasted for ten days at a time up to forty days and am preparing to do a thirty day fast now. Our entire church fasts. Many of our young people have done seven-day fasts with no food for that amount of time."

We're talking about the real item. Every Friday for the last two months Pastor Cacabelos and the intercessors from his church have walked around the congress building. As they are praying many times a spirit of weeping comes upon them.[1]

Héctor Ferreyra's son, Nicolás, is a student now at IBRP and mentioned the other day what had happened when he was six years old. That was when the Ferreyras first went to Neuquén with Steve Hill to plant the church. I was shocked to learn that their entire family fasted every other day, partly to be in prayer and partly because they had no food. Sacrifice is a part of any revival. No wonder that church grew from zero to 1,100 in one year!

FORGETTING TO DECLARE HIS ACTS

"Declare among the people his doings" (Ps. 9:11). Much of the staying power of revival has to do with giving testimony to what God is doing. Our conversation has so often been robberies and miracles, but not in that order.

We reserve regular times at IBRP for testimonies and always are hearing fresh and amazing things that God is doing in the lives of the students and through their ministry. In years of listening to these testimonies, I think I can remember two that were off base and devoid of true glorification material.

Today we were on our way up the stairs to class when I saw Leo Campbell, from Honduras. "Can I see the fillings God gave you last week?" I asked. Right there, between stair landings, he opened his mouth and showed me two beautiful new fillings. I was really close since I had the opportunity to be on the steps above him. I don't think I'll ever wary of things like this.

If we neglect declaring what God is doing, He will soon stop doing it. Part of living in revival is continuing to be amazed at God's work and loving demonstrations. Testifying of His grace and power should always be a joy.

Lagging in Missions

Argentina is experiencing its worst economic crisis ever. I heartily concur with Carlos Annacondia when he says that we had a window of opportunity for ten years with a peso as strong as the dollar, and we squandered that buying power on many other items except missions. Many feel that the country would still be experiencing financial blessing as a nation if the Christian church had stepped up and taken responsibility to send out more missionaries.

The longest-lasting revivals have always been in tandem with a heart for missions and vice-versa. The Jesuit historian, Johann Baegert, who wrote in the 1790s initial years of the Reformation: "We know why the Protestants are heretics: because they have no missions."[2] The Catholic church gained more converts through the missionary order movements than they lost by the Reformation. Unfortunately, many of the Reformation ministers and theologians who had thought through so clearly the concepts of "only faith" and "by grace alone" were not at all clear on the grace of God reaching out to a lost world. They theorized that each generation was responsible for its own salvation and that it was not the responsibility of the church.

Often when I teach missions here in Buenos Aires I state, "If you don't pay the light bill, they cut the electrical power. If we don't give generously to missions, God will also cut off

His power. It is not about us, but about reaching out to the world through us."

God has given a great deal to Argentina's church, but fire is designed to spread, not to be kept in so it burns itself out. The revival that has blessed Argentina means that Argentina has the life to extend itself to other nations and take that fire to them. I believe clearly that God is calling Argentina to a stronger missions emphasis and that without it, things may ultimately die.

DRINKING THE WATER

As well as sometimes being miserly in relation to missions, some pastors can also be miserly with their workers. At times they may not allow their workers to receive ministerial training because they fear losing them to the mission field or to a church plant.

How refreshing it was to hear one say, "I know that if I send five to train, God can give me fifty others." Argentine missionary Carlos Guerra is now working in Honduras, and God spoke to him audibly from the back seat of his car, "The work is mine and the workers are mine." If we cannot learn to relinquish control, we are lording it over the flock (see 1 Peter 5) and are in danger of negatively affecting God's revival.

So many of the churches have developed mighty men. They are like David's mighty men who did amazing exploits. (See 2 Samuel 23:8–17.) David was wise regarding this stewardship gift. His men loved their leader, so one day when he breathed a whimsical wish for water from a certain well near Bethlehem, the three mighty men decided to break through enemy lines and get it for him. When they returned with the water, David poured it out.

How surprising! Why did he do that? They had risked their lives for him and were willing to do so. The water was there, presented to him with pride. Why pour it out?

His response is telling. He basically says, "Far be it from me, O Lord, to do this! Is it not the blood of those who went at the risk of their lives?"

David felt checked by the Spirit in using his men for his own whims or the building of His own personal kingdom. Leaders who dominate others and selfishly take from them are out for personal gain. They are drinking the water for themselves.

Instead, it is meant to be shared, to be poured out for the work of the kingdom of God. People are supposed to be sent out, into missions, into church planting, and into the fulfill-ment of the dreams God has given them. We don't own anyone else. We don't dare even touch the water, let alone drink it.

FORGETTING ABOUT SOULS

Signs and wonders have as their main purpose the attrac-tion of sinners to Christ. They are the sound-and-light show that people see first and then come near to get the message. If the manifestations become the focus of everything, God will quickly quit working in this way. What He desires above all else is souls. He wants us to touch the lives of new people. He hopes that neighbors who find out their friend was healed or trans-formed will show up at church to find out how that happened.

The baptism of the Holy Spirit transforms us into power demonstrators who advance from Jerusalem to Samaria and on to the ends of the earth. We care what happens in Kosovo and in Bangladesh, and we are willing to get involved.

"God gave us ten years of joy and worship, and we did not understand the purpose was for evangelism. We neglected the streets, so the gangs and drug dealers took them back over." This was a solemn warning from Evangelist Carlos Annacondia.

Holding the fort; holding hands and singing together; holding on to key workers that should be thrust into the harvest; holding back on missions giving and burden; these are certain death rattles for a revival.

A revival is meant to breathe life into a dead body so it can live and be productive. It is not meant to be spent only on the saints, to be turned inward. Anything that is selfish does not bring long-term revival. Where the revival was focused egotistically, it dissipated. Where it was focused outward to produce new believers, it has thrived. Evangelism is always an outgrowth of a true revival.

LACK OF PRAYER

When prayer starts to dwindle, it is the sure sign that revival is waning. Here in Argentina, prayer continues to be a strong part of what God is doing. The pastors are critically aware of the need to continue to seek the Lord, to remain fervent in their love for Him. They lead their church to pray in many different formats and at various times. The services are usually bathed in prayer as people seek God while the services are occurring, often praying under the platform where the pastor is preaching and worship is being led.

Many of us are full of expectation that another strong wave of revival is on its way. The atmosphere at ministerial training centers many times reflects what God is about to do next. Though we emphasize prayer at IBRP, only personal hunger could produce what we are living this year. We hear students praying almost at all times—early in the morning and late at night. When they are not in class, someone is praying, either in the chapel, the small prayer room, or in one of the classrooms. The campus is very crowded, and one of the biggest challenges the students mention is finding a place to pray alone. What a good sign when people are frustrated that they can't find a place to seek the Lord's presence because every nook and cranny is occupied.

Losing the Centrality of Christ

The heart of the gospel is the incarnation of Christ, His atoning work of grace on the cross, and the resurrection. The message must remain the same, validated by the power of the Holy Spirit, enhanced by the gifts and manifestations, but still, "We preach Christ crucified" (1 Cor. 1:23). A close observation of the preaching of the key personalities in this revival will demonstrate that the gospel has not been changed or watered down. The cost of discipleship is still proclaimed very clearly as what it has always been: death to self and being crucified with Christ. (See Galatians 6:14.)

Manipulative spin-offs or attempts to take advantage of the energy of the revival have been observed to proclaim the motto, "Quit suffering." But the mainstream of God's river has continued to be biblical and doctrinally orthodox.

The Balancing Act

In the midst of revival, it seems that God works in certain ways to bring areas back into balance. During the 1990s when God's Spirit had taken us so by surprise, there were pastors who could not preach. They attempted to speak to the congregation or even adjust the microphone and could not. A holy disabling had come upon them, which made us very aware of why they thought the disciples were inebriated on the day of Pentecost. Worship services lasted five or six hours, sometimes going all night. Many times the leadership and congregation were so lost in worship that preaching was relegated to the next service.

I believe this was initially a corrective measure allowed by the Holy Spirit concerning the importance, value, and glory of God. The pulpit had become paramount. Most of the time, the preacher was introduced with these words, "Now the important part of the service has come." It was as if the speaker's preparation and personality were more important than worshiping God.

However, everything can go too far. During this time of finding ourselves lost in the presence of God, the pastor of a large church where I had spoken asked to accompany me to the car. His church had received so much from God and was growing very quickly. On the way he said, "Rocky, I'm going to have to go back to preaching the Word." A simple expository sermon that led the congregation to meditate for a time on a portion of the Bible had become the exception, and now the Lord was taking the pastor back to focus on the Word.

Another danger related to this particular balancing act is that the new cell-based structures leave out the systematic teaching of the Word, especially to children. Some means and methods of growth work well with those who do not have major responsibilities in the home, but they place major strains on family time, especially time with kids. We can't forget to shape our own children, especially with the Word of God.

Revival is basking in the presence of God, but it is also listening to His Word and obeying its principles. These both have to stay in their proper equilibrium.

Another balance that has to be maintained in revival is the new and the old, "Every scribe instructed concerning the kingdom of heaven is like a householder who brings out of his treasure things new and old" (Matt. 13:52, NKJV).

How important it is to know who we are in God, where we came from, and where He is taking us. We must sense our foundations, but we must also reach out and strain to find what God has for us in the future.

If the new generation doesn't know about Tommy Hicks, Kathryn Kuhlman, and Carlos Annacondia, they will miss so much depth and understanding and will be forced to experience from scratch their own hard lessons in faith and commitment.

Finally, we must maintain the balance between law and grace. It has taken the Argentine church decades to work past the strong legalism and emphasis on works that were taught in the beginning. Understanding grace is critical and has been one of the keys to continued growth in revival. The congregations that major on the minors ultimately lose out from the revival. Whether a woman wears slacks or make-up is not an issue anymore. This understanding has been an important key to growth.

Wrap-Up

God wants us to live in continual revival. The little book *Old Time Revivals,* by John Shearer states concerning R. A. Torrey that "in every church to which he ministered, he enjoyed a continuous revival. He taught his people that this great blessing is simply the restoration of the Church's health, and it is the Lord's will that His Body should enjoy robust and unfailing vigour, ever renewing its youth and drawing fresh strength from its trials."[3]

God's will for His church is vibrant life all of the time. He is not interested in merely refreshing us; He wants to empower us. His presence should be more than a morning mist that dissipates quickly; it should be a river that overwhelms us. Let's not be satisfied with a few short-lived mercy drops. Let's ask Him to send everything He has for us.

Living in a continuous revival is possible. But one has to skirt the potential dangers and pitfalls that come from the flesh and from Satan. As we seek to avoid the temptations and inertia and instead push ahead to what God has for us, we will continue to be blessed by His presence.

We need to keep listening. We must consider what He is doing and hear what He is saying to us.

10

What Is God Saying to Us?

WE LIVE IN a unique period in history. These are moments of unprecedented potential in communications and networking. Areas of the world that have been closed off from the gospel for centuries are now being penetrated by the light. Never before have so many nations been this involved in missions. At the same time there is an unprecedented number of distracting theories concerning the identity and methodology of the church.

At the time of the first advent of Jesus, the grand schemes of the Roman Empire were painted against a backdrop of pessimism and failure of nerve regarding the powers of man to work out his own future, and in the midst of this, Jesus came to earth. Likewise this age of a cacophony of chaotic voices and stress will surely be the backdrop for the Second Coming. We have very little time left and must make the best use of it. A critical element of "redeeming the time" is taking our cues from God and running toward the right goal.

We close our look at the Argentine revival by considering revival itself. What is God saying to us? Where do we go from here?

WHAT IS REVIVAL?

Some spend more time discussing and dissecting revival than seeking God for whatever He would desire to give their aching hearts. But one of the motivations of this book is to inspire us all to go beyond the talk and find the keys that so many have used consistently in their walk of living faith.

Revival is normality. Revival is biblical Christianity. Revival is the Book of Acts made up-to-date with each challenge and problem that is overcome. It is true that much of what Argentina has lived in the last five decades could be labeled an awakening. Those blessed and reached had not yet been made alive, and thus did not need reviving. But for the sake of fluid communication, let's just use the term as most Christians usually do: revival means God is moving in surprising ways in our lives and churches and is continually touching the lost through us.

Semantics can keep us from receiving all God has. What is the anointing? When is a move of God a true revival? What is a revivalist? What is an evangelist? We could go on and on with a myriad of questions which skirt the critical issue: What does God want for us? Are we willing to seek Him and to lay it all on the line for Him?

God is much more interested in our being true worshipers who seek His presence than in our being connoisseurs of revival. He wants us to abandon ourselves to His purposes, to get lost in His will.

In the midst of revival, we make God the center of everything. "If therefore thine eye be single, thy whole body shall be full of light" (Matt. 6:22), Jesus said. What does He mean? Undivided attention. An undivided heart. Realizing that everything we need is in Him.

WHY STUDY REVIVALS?

Why study revivals? Is it a mere curiosity fed by the desire to win at Spiritual Awakenings Trivia sometime? Absolutely not! We want to be ready for what God is going to do next. If we miss the obvious cues, we're going to be playing a piccolo solo after the concert is over.

"Been there, done that" is the attitude of some. They get bored and don't pay attention to what God is about to do. This approach will keep us from saying, "I won't leave this place until God blesses me. I want even more of Him."

Besides looking ahead, God wants us to stay attuned to the way He has done things in the past. We can dig up the old wells and find fresh water. (See Genesis 26:12–33.) There is beautiful consistency in His ways. If we have the attitude of Moses, we will look beyond His acts to knowing Him and serving Him on the basis of His grace. (See Psalm 103:7.) Moses got to know God for His ways, not just His deeds. He became a friend of God's.

We should all be students of revival. Through looking at what God has done in the past, we gain a deeper understanding of His ways. We learn from the mistakes of the leaders as well as from the positive things they did. We also are encouraged by the many wonderful moves of God that have occurred in the past. This is not merely an intellectual exercise, but it builds up our faith and gets us to the place where we say, "Lord, I'm desperate for you to move in my life."

R. Edward Miller once told me something about those early years here in Argentina, when God began to give them prophecy after prophecy of the powerful working He had prepared for the nation. Often the Lord would say to him, "All or nothing. All or nothing." What a passionate pursuit of the Lord!

Evan Robert's cry, "Lord, bend me," must be ours also. The motto of the Wales Revival became, "Bend the church and save the world."[1] John Knox's passionate exclamation was likewise, "Oh, God, give me Scotland or I'll die."

When we study revival, we see the deep hunger of so many men and women of God. It jars us out of our complacency and sends us running to Him with our arms open wide.

Revival Promises

After such a strong commitment, God begins to give visions and promises. It is important to value the things that the Holy Spirit tells us will happen. Without this faith we probably will not see revival.

Pastor Scataglini mentions both a strategy and a promise given him by the Holy Spirit starting in 1967 when he and his wife, Isabel, went to pastor in La Plata. They began with a plan. "The idea was to consolidate the homes of the believers, so there would not be a duality," said Scataglini. "I thought, here in the church is a lot of the glory of God, but in the home it is another lifestyle. The idea was to take the church to the home."

So they started with a snack or lunch and the owners of the house would invite their neighbors. "We saw they were getting converted," he continued, "and we realized this was a good evangelism method, more than just consolidating each home. So we came out with the slogan, 'In the temple and in every house' (reference to Acts 5:42). The houses began to grow, and we started calling them 'church houses or house churches,'" said Scataglini. "That's where the miracles started, too."

Within ten years of using this approach God had given new converts, and the church had grown to five hundred. "Today, when you say that number," smiled Scataglini, "it almost sounds trivial. But at that time if one accepted the Lord, it felt like getting drunk, out of joy."

Pastor Scataglini stated that after this God spoke to him and said that they would have an avalanche of people. "It was so strong," he said. "I would repeat it and repeat it to the church. 'We're going to have a flood. There will be an avalanche of people.' I was laughing at how they would laugh at me. They would look at me with their eyes wide, probably thinking, 'Poor guy. He wants to start a revival here.' I kept saying to the Lord, 'Why are You having me say this to the people if it is almost impossible that an avalanche of people will come?' For the church at that time, we had a good number. But God kept saying to me, 'An avalanche is on its way.'"

Little did Pastor Scataglini realize what a gigantic avalanche it would be, nor did he know how it would come. But God fulfilled what He said. There were so many other people with promises as well, wild ones, which hardly seemed possible at the time. Annacondia heard the Lord say, "Soon, soon, Argentina will be mine." Claudio Freidzon heard Him say, "The countries of the world." Hector Ferreyra heard Him say, "This is the time. Get prepared."

Thank God for those who heard His promises, took them seriously, believed Him, and acted on that faith. Without it, Argentina may never have seen revival.

Revival Demands a Clean House

One of our students stated this week that he doesn't know how he will be received when he returns to his own country, friends, and family. He says living in this move of God has changed him so much that he realizes he will not be able to go on as before. "Very few things used to bother me," he said. "I thought I was doing OK. But now I am so much more aware of who God is, and a lot of things bother me. I grieve when I displease Him." That is the expression of a person whose conscience has been sensitized by the Holy Spirit.

There are issues of holiness, those "little" sins and big ones that need to be cleared up. There is also a spiritual cleansing that needs to occur. Pastor Alberto Scataglini told of how the Spirit cleaned house in their church. "Every Saturday we were continually in prayer. We had prayer in the basement of this building," he said. "We did not allow any adult to come down unless they had been invited. Just the young people. Nobody understood that. But I knew that God wanted to heal and consolidate the young people. Many came and confessed their sins. There was a time that we placed a pillow on the floor, and we asked for those to come who wanted to be strengthened if they were feeling weak in a particular area. All of us identified with the need, the pain of that person, and we would pray for them. Many received the baptism of the Holy Spirit."

Pastor Scataglini continued with an interesting story. "We've seen how the Lord has worked concerning evil spirits so that what I'm going to say now is credible. It happened twice," he said. "On one occasion the young people went down to pray. I was still up here in the apartment, and they were already singing in the basement. When I got there, I sensed a strong evil presence in that place. I said to them, 'Stop singing. We need to pray.' We started interceding, and the young people had such an enthusiasm. That's when I understood the acts of the Apostles where it said they were of one heart. In a moment of the greatest emphasis and prayer intensity, suddenly something that came from the spiritual realm was manifested on earth. We have a sliding door that's all made out of glass in the basement. The glass on that door exploded when we said to this evil presence, 'You must leave.' And it also occurred with the glass back here in the apartment, a great big picture window. In that jovial lifestyle of the teens, we would say, 'Those demons didn't have time to open the door.'"

Pastor Scataglini concluded his account by stating, "Probably the most important thing is that the glass from that door fell at the feet of a girl who had come for the first time. She was the niece of a well-recognized witch here in the city, and the glass all fell at her feet. We were all praying for the conquest, that God would give us the power."

In the midst of revival, God cleans people up. Repentance is necessary, and it paves the way for effective spiritual warfare so the move of God can go forward right into the enemy camp. Satan must flee, and God takes charge.

Find Your Place in the Revival

There were many contemporaries of Evan Roberts who lost out on participating in one of the most powerful revivals ever. They had other things going; personal things; important things that could not wait.

David Matthews, in his book *I Saw the Welsh Revival,* recounts his first experience with that great move of God. He and his voice teacher had determined to go to the theater one evening but then changed their minds and headed for the revival. "We walked and talked of the revival and our conversation was perhaps unwise, because neither of us had ever witnessed a revival. Our opinions were, therefore, worthless. Like many others who lived before us, we freely ventilated our vain thoughts. Then something happened. My friend decided that he would proceed no further. My persuasive powers availed nothing. After lengthy debate, he decided he would return to his studio. Equally obstinate, I determined that nothing would hold me back. Although 'the revival' brought blessing to thousands of his compatriots, the Spirit of God, as far as one could impartially discern, left my friend severely alone. There was no evidence that 'the powers of the world to come' had affected him in the least. Had I turned back with him, would I be writing these reminiscences?"[1]

Each person must decide for themselves where they will stand in relation to the revival. Will criticism be the order of the day? Stand back; wait and see? Dabble and test? Jump in? Lead? Whatever the choice is, we will reap from that choice.

We all have to put aside those opinions from the past and allow God to do His new work. It gives me great joy to say that many denominational leaders put their prejudices away and joined the revival. Most of the pastors from many of these Christian fellowships are Spirit-filled, worship freely, and flow in the gifts of the Spirit. There was a time when many of them had to defer and send the demon-possessed to their Pentecostal pastor friends for help. No more. They are now totally enabled by God to deal with the situations. They have sought and received the baptism in the Holy Spirit.

Pastor Alberto Aranda had been invited to teach pastoral theology at a night Bible school in a non-Pentecostal church. The pastor of the church had asked him to write up all his notes word for word beforehand, so he could go over them and avoid any Pentecostal influence and the ensuing trouble. Alberto was happy to acquiesce. However, to everyone's surprise, as he so carefully read his notes, many of the students began to receive the baptism in the Holy Spirit and to pray in tongues, right in class!

The pastor determined that he would like to get to know Aranda's church better and a date was set when he could go there to preach. Everything went fine, including an invitation for Alberto to speak at his church. As they were standing on the sidewalk at the door of the church, some young ladies from the church yelled goodbye from a block away. "Good night, pastor!" they sang out cheerfully. Aranda raised his hand to wave goodbye—and the girls fell down. The denominational pastor immediately said, with some trepidation, "When you come to my church, don't do that. We have a lot of traffic that goes by, and it might be dangerous."

When Aranda did go to his church, the pastor said, "Let me know if there is anything we can do for you." Alberto asked for them to move the plants on the platform so the congregation could see him.

As he stepped behind the pulpit, the Lord spoke to him, "There are five thieves present. Call them up to the front."

"But Lord," he argued, "I'm a guest here. It is the first time I have spoken in this church."

"Call them up," came the insistent impression from the Holy Spirit.

Obediently, before making any introductory remarks, Aranda stated, "There are five people present who are involved in stealing. God wants you to come forward and repent." Then he waited.

In very little time, five people ran up to the altar, weeping profusely and repenting of their sins.

Upon seeing so many demonstrations of God's power, the pastor friend sought the baptism in the Holy Spirit and began to move in the gifts. Taking his place in the revival cost him dearly. He was expelled from his denomination and lost his position as a national evangelist. But his church grew ten-fold, and God is surely pleased with him for risking it and stepping up.

REVIVAL BRINGS ENJOYMENT

Revival brings many things to appreciate. One is that there is a great pleasure in being with God's people. Revival is about the church gathering in deep *koinonia* and finding God's purposes together. The center of life during a revival is the church. The mall can wait. Hobbies and sports take their places at the bottom of the list of priorities. The people of God make their agenda fit the church and not vice versa.

Another enjoyment revival brings is the fruit of revival, which are new lives born into the Lord's kingdom. Personalities are transformed, bringing more tenderness, sensitivity, and carefulness with each other and with God. The fruit of revival is "peace, and joy in the Holy Ghost" (Rom. 14:17). People are sweeter, more patient, and more loving.

Revival also brings an enjoyment of God's power. What could be more exciting than seeing God heal someone's feet or make varicose veins disappear? Watching limbs grow out is a lot more exciting than just about anything I can think of. Headaches disappear, hernias are healed, and teeth receive divine fillings. These evidences of God's grace have been normal here in the last twenty years. A church in revival expects miracles, waits on God to act, and then they see Him do the impossible.

It is not a pride thing. It is a matter of joining Him and participating with our faith in what He wants to do. The Lord's words are still in effect today, "Greater *works* than these shall he do; because I go unto my Father" (John 14:12, emphasis added). How do we do those greater works? Through the power of the Holy Spirit in conjunction with our faith.

Additionally, in a revival God brings enjoyment of His own presence and personality. Revival is not about manifestations—it is about God. It is not just about demonstrations of power, it is really about the Creator and His love. The Lord yearns for a church that will seek to know Him better, love Him more, worship Him with abandon, desire Him wholeheartedly, and relax in His presence without a hurried agenda.

REVIVAL DEMANDS RISK AND FAITH

Pastor Carlos Mraida, theologian, denominational leader, and pastor of the Church of the Center in Buenos Aires, has an interesting comment in his book, *Socorro, Señor, Mi Iglesia se Renovó y no la Entiendo* (*Help, Lord, My Church Got Renewed and I Do Not Understand It*).

"What are falling, laughter, weeping, and the sensation of tickling?" Mraida asks. "They are simply external signs from God to awaken and affirm our faith. Why? Because in His infinite wisdom, and in His enormous respect for our freedom, He has determined that His intervention requires the exercise of our faith."

Indeed, it is important that we move past our own self-consciousness and look at God. It takes faith to exercise the gifts of the Spirit the way God desires. However, the gifts have been handed to us merely to give away to someone else. If we do not deliver them, the people will never receive and be able to open their gift.

In his book Pastor Mraida mentions a lady who said to him, "Pastor, pray for my friend. She is paralyzed and can barely move from the pain."

He shared, "I lifted my hand to place it on the woman and pray for healing, but the Holy Spirit showed me that she was harboring hatred and resentment. Then I said to the lady from my church, 'The cause of her sickness is the hatred and the resentment that are in her heart. Help her to forgive and take out of her heart those negative feelings.'

"Later while I was still greeting the people, I noticed the two women leaving. The one who had been paralyzed was moving about freely, with a big smile on her face. It was not necessary to pray for her physical healing."

Giving a prophetic word demands risk-taking faith. I know of someone who recently told a story while she was preaching about a man she had witnessed to on an airplane ride. He had looked like "Mr. All-Together," a professional man in a business suit, but as they talked, she told him about Jesus, and he was so open, having recently gone through a painful divorce and now desperately missing his boys.

After she finished the message in which she had related this story of "Mr. All-Together," she was ministering at the altar and felt led by the Spirit to say to another man, "In so many ways you are just like that man in the story who was on the airplane." She knew nothing about him, and it took faith for her to say this.

He started to weep, realizing that God was speaking directly to him. When He stood up, he said, "You're right. I look like I have it all together in my suit here, but inside I'm a mess." Later she found out he was a psychologist, divorced, with a son. God reached down into that man's life. He knew God loved him, and there was much encouragement in the word from the Lord.

In order to do these sorts of things, though, we must go beyond caring if we will be embarrassed and merely do our best to listen to God's voice, believe and obey. It is not about us. It is about Him.

Revival stirs up the gifts of the Holy Spirit, but we must choose to operate in them. In 1 Timothy 4:14, there is a strong word from Paul to Timothy about this matter, showing us that the responsibility is ours. The Holy Spirit's power and enablement are available. It is up to us to stir up what He has planted so deeply within us.

In 2 Timothy 1:6, it states, "Fan into flame the gift of God, which is in you" (NIV). Paul had prayed for Timothy earlier, and he knew there were gifts inside of him. God wants to use us in the gifts of the Spirit, too. The flame is there. We just have to fan it so it will burst forth in all of its brightness.

God Uses Children and Youth in Revival

We are in winter vacation. Since we are in the southern hemisphere, these two weeks of vacation take place in July. Most churches have youth retreats during these days. This week I was invited to speak at a retreat where only eighty young people had signed up. Four hundred showed up!

The organizers ran out of mattresses, so they just pushed all of them together and made do. They preferred to have everyone suffer a little rather than exclude any of these young people. The first night they were all up praying until four o'clock in the morning.

We are facing the challenge of a new generation that needs it own personal experience with Pentecost and revival. It is not enough simply to hear about it. They need to have it for themselves.

Martha Lesperance, missionary to the teenagers of Argentina, has seen Castillo del Rey, King's Castle ministry grow in a mere three years to two thousand teenagers involved. The students are constantly out on the streets and plazas evangelizing through music and drama. Many of them are also very involved in moving in the gifts of the Holy Spirit. One formerly shy young man went to his church and prophesied for an hour!

Martha mentioned that at a retreat the young people sat around the campfire and prayed all night in freezing temperatures. They were so involved in what God's Spirit was doing that they were unaware of the cold.

Freddy Arguello, one our IBRP students from the Province of Misiones near Brazil, had some amazing events to share in a recent letter. "A girl had leukemia and was in serious condition, about to die in the hospital. I went to pray for her and two days later she was released. She was totally healed for the glory of the Lord. Hernias have disappeared. A lady with a stomach ulcer came to one of our home meetings. After we prayed, she went and had the medical tests done, and the doctors found nothing. A woman had cancer of the uterus which had spread all over her body, plus an issue of blood. We went to the hospital to see her. I quoted the episode where Jesus healed a woman who was suffering from the same thing she was. As I spoke, she believed and after praying profoundly, the hemorrhaging stopped. When they gave her the medical exams, the large tumor in the uterus and all other cancer were gone. The only thing that appeared was a small tumor on the uterus, and it was benign.

"We have a notebook full of the testimonies that we have written down," continued Freddy. "Each person who prays makes comments. The truth is that the home meetings have gone way beyond our expectations."

Thank God for a pastor who has allowed this young man to be involved in the revival.

God Is Particularly Creative in Revival

We must be willing to adapt our structures to the move of God and to the needs of people. Guillermo Prein's church found that many of the older saints had difficulty attending church at night because of the lack of security in these days. He also realized that there were women whose unsaved husbands were gone to work during the day. Others were assigned to the evening shift and so couldn't come to church during those hours. As a result the church leadership determined to hold a service to meet these needs at two o'clock every day.

One of the new structures used in many churches is the "weekend encounter" where a group will go on retreat for three days and spend from morning until past midnight in prayer, praise, worship, and teaching. Many pastors find that new converts grow as much in one weekend as they do in a year of merely attending a large church.

God also is creative when it comes to music and the arts. Revival seems to bring out new worship songs, fresh beats and rhythms, novel approaches, and expression. Artists are set free to paint, write, sculpt, design, choreograph, and express themselves in drama.

It seems that in revival God asks people to watch carefully, to discern, to be ready and "instant" in doing or saying what is needed at the moment. He asks them not to get bogged down with the cares of the world and routine, but to listen and be open.

How often we have seen the leadership just "go with the flow" of God's working. Instead of stopping to write a theological treatise, they merely observed what was happening and went with it. Of course, they sorted out the human element, guarded against deception, and kept to the Word, but there was no time to be armchair theologians. Everyone was too busy keeping up with the next great act of God.

Pastor Alberto Scataglini speaks of a fantastic miracle brought about by the Lord in a creative fashion. "A lady who came to the evangelistic crusade," he recalled, "put some clothing on the table provided during the campaign. It was for her husband with paralysis who was home in a wheelchair, but she had left the window open so that he could hear what was happening in the campaign." Carlos Annacondia always wanted the volume to be as high as possible; everything to the max. Some people got healed six blocks away because they could hear what was going on.

This man was listening, too. When his wife came back, she said, "Well, I took these socks. Put them on." He put the socks on, and he started crying out, "I'm burning, I'm burning." He felt it so strongly that he started kicking his feet, but he had gotten up out of the chair, and he started tap dancing all over. God had healed him!

Revival Builds Unity and Spills Out Into the Community

A critical piece of the revival puzzle is unity. Pastor Alberto Scataglini speaks of the risks he took at the beginning of that pace-setting campaign in La Plata. He believes that at first it was an awakening, and then with time it turned into a revival. He sees an awakening occurring when one congregation is open to God's work. Then it becomes a revival when all the congregations of a city are involved and associated for that purpose and it spreads. When the whole Republic of Argentina was the platform for this ministry, it became a revival.

"It was very challenging and difficult here for six to eight months," Scataglini remembers. "I said, 'Lord, this city is so hard. The evangelist has been here for a long time.' And the answer I had from the Lord was this, 'It is not the people. It is the pastors.' Does that say anything to you?" asks Scataglini.

"When we lived that enthusiasm and faith, I wrote on a piece of paper a list of all the churches," Scataglini continues. "I placed it in the newspaper of the city, and I printed up a lot of pamphlets with the list on them and handed them out all over the place. They listed the address of all the churches, inviting people to the campaign."

Some pastors came to the campaign, but to insult him. "They asked me who was I to place their church name in there without their permission," said Scataglini. "I answered, 'You're right. I'm sorry, but I didn't want you to miss out on this blessing.'" There were six campaigns in all and by the sixth all the congregations participated. God ultimately brought unity.

The revival in Mar del Plata was something totally out of the ordinary. In the schools they would sing choruses from the campaign. It was a time for a lot of work. "When we would be called to the hospitals to visit," stated Scataglini, "we were all seeing so many miracles of cancer and lungs being healed and so forth. As we'd go into the hospitals, we'd see the nurses and the people who cared for the place singing the choruses of the campaign."

Even in the schools the children went out on the playgrounds, and their play was related to the campaigns and acting like they were in church. A lady who directed a school called the father of one of the students and said, "Something strange is happening with your son."

The father answered, "What happened? Has he been misbehaving?"

"Not really, but at recess, he makes everybody line up and he places his hand on them and they fall down. What's happening with your son?"

The child was not just pretending; he was demonstrating the power of God.

REVIVAL RESULTS IN REACHING OUT TO THE LOST

Revival is not intended to stay inside the church. Jesus told His disciples to "go into all the world and preach the gospel." *Go out* is the opposite of *come in*. Revival stirs the church, refreshes it, and brings it alive again for a reason: so it can more effectively do what it was intended to do all along.

A "revived" church that does not result in outreach is well nigh impossible. When God moves, people get excited, and they tell their friends. In his book *The King Describes His King-*

dom, Rick Howard mentions a pungent moment while he was speaking at a large church in Buenos Aires. He was talking about Matthew 13 and said that the good seed are the children of the kingdom. He preached that fruit cannot be produced unless those lives are planted in the world. Carlos Annacondia was sitting on the platform and was impacted by the Word. He stated, "Here we are building bigger and bigger barns to store the harvest, when God wants it to be planted in the world."

God is telling us to spread out the seed so we can see even more come into the kingdom! Many in Argentina feel that it is harvest time in this country and that the Lord will bring even more into the kingdom. We are expecting thousands more to see the Savior with new eyes, and the churches are preparing for this to happen. We don't want to lose the harvest after it has been reaped. Further, God is drawing Argentina to look beyond itself to other countries that desperately need the fire of revival.

Recently Brazilian Evangelist Jaco Torres spoke to our students. At the end of a very colorful message he shared a vision God had given him. At first, he saw a woman standing with her children, and they were all crying. Then he saw them smiling and happy, and he was being lifted up toward a huge flag above him. Suddenly a window opened in the flag and his head went through the window to the other side. He stared at wheat fields as far as the eye could see, ready for harvest. "I wish that flag that I saw had been the Brazilian flag," he said. "But it was blue-white-blue, the Argentine flag. I believe that after all of the suffering of 2001, God is going to bless Argentina and use the country mightily as a window to the harvest."

WRAP-UP

God wants His river to flood out to the whole world. May He find us faithful to participate according to the parameters of His will. He is giving dreams and visions right now, and He wants every single one of us involved.

We need to be alert, expectant, pure, ready, and flexible. Right now we need to be open about what He wants to do next so we can be in step with it. We should be listening carefully.

When Jesus came to earth the first time, so many missed Him, though they had been waiting for the Messiah. This was especially true of the religious folk. God help us as we approach His Second Coming, so we are more in tune and don't miss what He wants to do now. It is a powerful time of preparation.

Revival has been coming to the country of Argentina for decades. Our God has saved, transformed, healed, and shown Himself to be the King of kings. We are expectant for more; something new and fresh; another strong wave. May it flow in and then go out—touching many others. And I pray this account of what the Lord has done will touch you, dear reader, as well. We serve a mighty God who deserves our praise for all of His mighty work. His presence is everything.

Afterword

I T HAS BEEN amazing to watch the process of correction and translation of this manuscript. God has used the testimonies in surprising ways.

I asked five different IBRP students to read two chapters each. One of them, David Albert, read through the entire book in three days. God's power fell, and he ended up on the floor various times as he read of the tremendous acts of our Lord.

Cynthia Herrera was finding the names in the entire manuscript to seek permission to publish the different testimonies. A fire began to take hold of her, and she determined to finish a certain day. Taking only ten minutes for lunch, she continued to read. A girlfriend came to pick her up at 5:00 p.m., but she asked her to wait—until 8:00 p.m. "Then something happened to me that I had been desiring for a long time," Cynthia shares. She took courage and with her friend prepared many evangelistic booklets, taping a piece of candy to each. Then these two well-dressed young ladies went out and started stopping public buses, asking the driver permission to speak to the passengers on board and to distribute the literature. The first driver said, "No, you'll just be wasting your time. There's hardly anyone on the bus." But they persisted and ended up sharing testimony and literature on various full buses that day.

Ronald Barba was translating the manuscript into Spanish and states that God spoke to his heart. "His voice through these teachings made great changes in my life, and consequently in the life of my family." Sometimes God's presence was so strong he had to quit writing. He is sharing some of these principles in various churches where he holds music and worship seminars.

Students and pastors in Albania have been blessed by the testimonies, according to missionaries Rob and Diana Nelson. North Central University used the manuscript in one of its revivals classes recently as did Southwestern Assemblies of God University.

I am deeply grateful to Creation House for accepting to publish the manuscript. The dream of many years is coming true! Virginia Maxwell as production manager has been very helpful and encouraging.

So many fresh testimonies from pastors and our students are coming up now that I have already started hoping for a sequel to this book.

—Rocky Grams
Buenos Aires, Argentina
July 28, 2006

Bibliography

Abregú, Sergio. Interview by author, 2004.

———. Interview with the revival class of North Central University, Dr. Carolyn Tennant, and Dr. David Nichols, 1999.

Annacondia, Carlos. Interview with the revival class of North Central University and Dr. Carolyn Tennant, 2004.

———. *Oíme bien, Satanás!* Colombia: Bethany/Caribe, 1997.

———. *Campagna San Martín mensaje de salvación No. 2.* Buenos Aires: El Verbo, 1985.

———. *Campagna Moreno-Beccar.* Buenos Aires: Organo Informativo Equipo Evangelístico Mensaje de Salvación, 1985.

———. *Listen to Me, Satan! Exercising Authority Over the Devil in Jesus' Name.* Lake Mary, FL: Charisma House, 1998.

Annacondia, Ruth. E-mail, assistant to Carlos Annacondia, July, 2006.

Aranda, Alberto. Interview by author, 2003, 2005.

Arevalo, Andrés, Ed. *Campagna 84 mar del plata Jesús te ama: Hoy en el mundo mar del plata.* Buenos Aires: Assemblies of God Field Focus, 1985.

"Avivamiento." *Edifiquemos* 10, no. 16 (2004).

Barba, Ronald. Interview by author, 2006

Barbieri, Esteban. Interview by Internet, 2004.

———. Telephone interview by author, 2005.

Bartleman, Frank. *Azusa Street.* New Kensington: Whitaker House, 1982.

Basso, Alfredo. Interview by author, 2006.

Beckham, William A. *The Second Reformation: Reshaping*

the Church for the 21st Century. Houston, TX: Touch Publications, 1995.

Benítez, Oscar. Message in Instituto Bíblico Río de la Plata chapel, 2005.

Bueno, John. "Revival in Latin America," *Pentacostal Evangel.* Springfield Missouri, January 6, 2002.

Bühne, Wolfgang. *Explosión Carismática.* Terrassa, Spain: Editorial Clie, 1994.

Cacauelos, Ricardo. Note, July 10, 2006.

Carníval, Osvaldo. Interview with the revival class of North Central University, Dr. Carolyn Tennant, and Dr. David Nichols, 1999.

————. Interview with the revival classes of North Central University and Assemblies of God Theological Seminary, Dr. Carolyn Tennant, and Dr. David Nichols, 2000.

————. Interview with the revival class of North Central University and Dr. Carolyn Tennant, 2004.

————. Interview with Dr. Carolyn Tennant and Rocky Grams, July 2004.

Carrillo, Miguel Angel. Interview by author, September 5, 2006.

Churruarín, Juan José. *El precio de la unción: Pasos en la dimensión del poder de Dios.* Miami: Editorial Vida, 1999.

Confederación Espírita Panamericana C.E.P.A, http://www.cepanet.org/espanhol/cepa.php (accessed 9/4/06).

Contreras, Gilbert. Interview by author, 2005.

Coppin, Ezra. *Guns, Guts and God.* San Diego: Production House Publishers, 1976.

Crónicas del Fuego. E-mail, unpublished testimonies from Puerta del Cielo Church, La Plata, 2005.

Deiros, Pablo, A. and Carlos Mraida. *Latinoamérica en llamas: Historia y creencias del movimiento religioso mas impresionante de todos los tiempos.* Nashville: Editorial Caribe, 1994.

Dempster, Murray W., Byron Klaus, and Douglas Peterson. *The Globalization of Pentecostalism: A Religion Made to Travel.* Irvine, CA: Regnum Books, 1999.

Di Crescienzo, Juan. Interview by author, 2005.

———. Interview by Cintia Herrera and Alejandro Isaguirre, 2006.

DiTrolio, Rocco. Interview by author, 1992.

Edifiquemos magazine, "Misiones," año V, número 6, Buenos Aires: Departamento de Educación Cristiana, Unión de las Asambleas de Dios, March 1994.

Exley, Don. "Victories in the Southern Cone," *Pentecostal Evangel*, 1997.

———. "Revival Produces Passion for the Lost," *Pentecostal Evangel*, November 1997.

Ferreyra, Hector. Messages in Instituto Biblico Rio de la Plata chapel, 1998–2005.

Forni, Floreal, Fortunato Mallimaci, and Luis A. Cárdenas. *Guía de la diversidad religiosa de Buenos Aires.* Buenos Aires: Editorial Biblos, 2003.

Freidzon, Betty. *Sorprendida por Dios.* Lake Mary, FL: Casa Creación, 2005.

Freidzon, Claudio. Interview with the revival class of North Central University, Dr. Carolyn Tennant, and Dr. David Nichols, 1999.

———. Interview with the revival classes of North Central University and Assemblies of God Theological Seminary and Dr. Carolyn Tennant, 2000.

———. Interview with the revival class of North Central University and Dr. Carolyn Tennant, 2004.

———. Interview with Dr. Carolyn Tennant and Rocky Grams, 2004.

———. *Espíritu Santo, tengo hambre de ti.* Nashville, TN: Betania, 1996.

———. *Tesoro en vasos de barro.* Miami: Caribe/Betania, 1999.

Gardiner, Allen. *El martir de tierra del fuego* from the book *The Story of Commander Allen Gardiner.* Temuco: Alianza.

————. "Últimos documentos el Capitán Allen Gardiner," Colección documentos, dirigida por G. Baez, Mexico: Editorial Jákez, 1959.

Garduano Silva, Pablo. *Pasión que consume: Vida y ministerio de Alberto Mottesi*. Miami: Editorial Unilit, 1993.

Gebel, Dante. Message in Instituto Bíblico Río de la Plata chapel, 1999.

————. Interview with the revival class of North Central University, Dr. Carolyn Tennant, and Dr. David Nichols, 1999.

————. Interview by Internet, 2005.

————. *Pasión de multitudes: La pasión genuina de miles de jóvenes por la santidad*. Miami: Caribe/Betania, 1999.

Geddert, Ron. "Revival Stirs Argentine Mennonites," *Charisma* magazine, April, 1994.

Gee, Donald. *The Fruit of the Spirit* (New revised edition). Springfield, MO: Ghioni, Andrés. Interview by author, 2005.

González, Damián. Interview by author, 1998.

————. Interview with the revival class of North Central University, Dr. Carolyn Tennant, and Dr. David Nichols, 1999.

————. Interview with the revival classes of North Central University and Assemblies of God Theological Seminary, Dr. Carolyn Tennant, and Dr. David Nichols, 2000.

————. Interview with the revival class of North Central University and the author, 2002.

González, Norma. Interview with the evangelism class of Instituto Bíblico Río de la Plata and the author, 2005.

González, Nino. *Manteniendo Pentecostés pentecostal: Hacia un avivamiento permanente*. Miami, FL: Editorial Vida, 1998.

Gorbato, Viviana. *La Argentina embrujada*, Buenos Aires: Editorial Atlantida, 1996.

Grams, Nathan. Interview by author, 1994.

Grams, Rocky and Sherry. Assemblies of God missionary newsletters, 1979–2004.

―――. *In Awe in Argentina* e-mail testimonies. March 21, 2001–March 25, 2005.

Hill, Steve. Interview by author, 1998.

Hiatt, Ralph. Interview by author, 2005.

Horn, Ken. Conversation with Claudio Freidzon, "Outpouring in Argentina," *Pentecostal Evangel*, February 8, 1998.

Howard, Rick. *The King Describes His Kingdom: A Revolutionary Look at Matthew 13 in Light of Contemporary Times*. Woodside, CA: Naioth, 2003.

Instituto Bíblico Río de la Plata, tapes of student testimonies in chapel, 1995–2005.

Ibarra, Pedro. Interview with revivals class of North Central University, Assemblies of God Theological Seminary, Dr. Carolyn Tennant, and Dr. David Nichols, 2004.

―――. E-mail, June 26, 2006.

Jakob, Johann and S. J. Baegert. *Observation in Lower California*. Berkeley, CA: University of California Press, reprint edition, 1979.

Jenkins, Philip. *The Next Christendom: The Coming of Global Christianity*. New York: Oxford University Press, 2002.

Junco, Fernando. Interview by author, 2004.

Kolihuinka Navarro, Domingo. Message in Instituto Bíblico Río de la Plata chapel, 2000.

Lampan, J. Conrad. *The Second Call: Argentine Revival* e-mail newsletter, 2004.

Lesperance, Martha. Interview by author, 2003.

Luciani, Mara, assistant to Pastor Zucarelli. E-mail, July 3, 2006.

Maccio, Esteban. Interview by author, 2003.

―――. Message in Instituto Bíblico Río de la Plata chapel, 2003.

Matthews, David. *I Saw the Welsh Revival* (new, revised

edition). Pensacola, FL: Christian Life Books, 2002.

Miller, Edward. Interview with the revival classes of North Central University and Assemblies of God Theological Seminary, Dr. Carolyn Tennant, and Dr. David Nichols, 2000.

———. Message in Instituto Bíblico Río de la Plata chapel, 2000.

———. *Thy God Reigneth: The Story of Revival in Argentina.* Fairburn, GA: Peniel Outreach Ministries, Inc., 1964.

"Misiones." *Edifiquemos* 5, no. 6 (1994).

Molina, Marcelo and Corina. Interview by author, 2000.

Montemurro, Silvia, assistant to Pastor Omar Olier. E-mail, July 2006.

Mraida, Carlos. *Socorro Señor, mi iglesia se renovó y no la entiendo.* Buenos Aires, Argentina: Ediciones Certeza, 2004.

Muñoz, Edgardo. Interview with the revival class of North Central University, Dr. Carolyn Tennant, and Dr. David Nichols, 1999.

———. Interview with the revival classes of North Central University and Assemblies of God Theological Seminary, Dr. Carolyn Tennant, and Dr. David Nichols, 2000.

———. Interview with the revival class of North Central University and Dr. Carolyn Tennant, 2004.

Muñoz, Edgardo. Interview by author, 2004, 2006.

Murillo, Mario. *Fresh Fire: When You Are Finally Serious About Power in the End Times.* Danville, CA: Anthony Douglas Publishing, 1991.

Nicholson, Richard. Interview by author, 2003.

Nervegna, Eliana. Interview with the revival classes of North Central University and Assemblies of God Theological Seminary, Dr. Carolyn Tennant, and Dr. David Nichols, 2000.

———. E-mail, 2006.

Nostas, Silvina. Testimony at Instituto Bíblico Río de la Plata, 2001.

Ogden, Greg. *The New Reformation*. Grand Rapids, MI: Zondervan, 1990.

Petersen, Douglas. *Not By Might Nor By Power: A Pentecostal Theology of Social Concern in Latin America*. Irvine, CA: Oxford Regnum, 1996.

Prein, Guillermo. Interview with the revival class of North Central University, Dr. Carolyn Tennant, and Dr. David Nichols, 1999, 2000.

Ibid., 2004.

———. Message to the General Conference of the Unión de las Asambleas de Dios, 2003.

———. E-mail, August 6, 2006.

Pedrozo, Antonio. Message in Instituto Bíblico Río de la Plata chapel, 2003.

Pratney, Winkie. *Revival: Principles to Change the World*. Springdale, CA: Whitaker House, 1983.

"Revista informativa de las Asambleas de Dios." *Avance* 13, no 2 (1999).

Rey, Alberto. Interview by author, 2000.

———. Interview with the revival class of North Central University and Dr. Carolyn Tennant, 2004.

Rey de Reyes Enfoque, *El Fuego del Avivamiento se Encendió en Ecuador*, año 2, número 11. Buenos Aires, El Mundo Para Cristo Producciones, 1997.

Romay, Alberto. Interview by author, 2000, 2004.

———. Interview with the revival class of North Central University and Dr. Carolyn Tennant, 2004.

Romay, Milena. Interview by author, 2004.

Salazar, Horacio. Message in Instituto Bíblico Río de la Plata chapel, 1999.

Samorano, Coalo. "Jesús, eres mi buen Pastor," Grupo CanZion, 1998.

Santos, Guillermo. E-mail, July 17, 2006.

Savenko, Alejandro. Interview by author, 2004, 2005.

Scataglini, Alberto. Interview with the revival class of North Central University, Dr. Carolyn Tennant, and Dr. David Nichols, 1999.

————. Interview with revivals class of North Central University, Dr. Carolyn Tennant, 2004.

————. Message at Rey de Reyes Church Breakthrough Conference, 2004.

Scataglini, Kathleen. E-mail, May 11, 2005.

Scataglini, Sergio. *The Fire of His Holiness*. Ventura, CA: Renew/Gospel Light, 1999.

Seselovsky, Alejandro. *Cristo llame ya: Crónicas de la avanzada evangélica en la Argentina*. Buenos Aires: Grupo Editorial Norma, 2005.

Shearer, John. *Old Time Revivals*. Philadelphia, PA: The Million Testaments Campaign, 1932.

Silberbeib, Pablo. Message in Instituto Bíblico Río de la Plata chapel, 2001.

————. Interview by author, 2001.

Skidmore, Thomas E. and Peter H. Smith. *Modern Latin America*. New York: Oxford University Press, 2001.

Sosa, Eduardo and Edith. Interview in a Missions Latin American Advanced School of Theology class, 1999.

Sosa, Eduardo. Interview in a Missions class at Instituto Bíblico Río de la Plata, 2000.

Stamateas, Bernardo. Interview by author, 2002.

Stokes, Louis. *Historia del movimiento pentecostal en la Argentina*. Buenos Aires: Grancharoff, 1968.

Stokes, Louie W. *The Tommy Hicks Revival*. Unpublished diary. Buenos Aires, 1954.

Stormont, George. *Wigglesworth: A Man Who Walked With God*. Tulsa, OK: Harrison House, 1989.

Strang, Stephen. "Revival Surges in Argentina," *Charisma* magazine, April, 1989.

Strejilevich, Sergio. http://www.pagina12.com.ar/2001/suple/futuro/01-01/ 01-01-20/nota_a.htm.

Tennant, Carolyn. Interview by author, 2004.

————. Revivals class held at River Plate Bible Institute in conjunction with the Breakthrough Conference at King of Kings church, 2000.

Towns, Elmer and Douglas Porter. *The Ten Greatest*

Revivals Ever: From Pentecost to the Present. Ann Arbor, MI: Servant Publications, Vine Books, 2000.

"Una multitud en el Obelisco, por el tango y por una cruzada...quién es Dante Gebel?" *Diario Clarín.* December 13, 1998.

Unión de las Asambleas de Dios. *Memoria Anual.* 1984.

Unión de las Asambleas de Dios. *Circular Número 263.* 1985.

Wagner, C. Peter. *On the Crest of the Wave: Becoming a World Christian.* Ventura, CA: Regal Books, 1983.

———. *Spiritual Power and Church Growth: Lessons From the Amazing Growth of Pentecostal Churches in Latin America.* Lake Mary, FL: Strang Communications Company, 1986.

Wagner, C. Peter and Pablo Deiros. *The Rising Revival: Firsthand Accounts of the Incredible Argentina Revival.* Ventura, CA: Renew Books, Gospel Light, 1998.

Walker, Luisa Jeter. *Siembra y cosecha: resena histórica de las Asambleas de Dios en Argentina, Bolivia, Chile, Paraguay, Perú y Uruguay.* Miami, FL: Editorial Vida, 1992.

Walz, Brad. "Lessons From a 'Strange South American' Revival." Unpublished article, 1993.

Walz, Brad and Rhonda. Interview by Dr. Carolyn Tennant and the North Central University revivals class, 2004.

Ward, Robert. "Argentina: Heaven Comes Down as Churches Experience the Presence of God," *Joy.* n.d.

Warner, Wayne E., ed. *Revival! Touched by Pentecostal Fire, Eyewitnesses to the Early Twentieth-century Pentecostal Revival.* Tulsa, OK: Harrison House, 1978.

Wells, H. G. *The Outline of History: The Whole Story of Man.* Garden City, NY: Garden City Books, 1961.

Notes

2 —— WAVES OF REVIVAL

1. Sergio Strejilevich Web page. See http://www.pagina12
.com.ar/2001/suple/Futuro/01-01/01-01-20/nota_a
.htm (accessed August 25, 2006).
2. Confederación Espírita Panamericana C. E. P. A.,
"History," http://cepanet.org/espanhol/cepa.php
(accessed September 4, 2006).
3. Viviana Gorbato, *La Argentina Embrujada* (Buenos
Aires: Editorial Atlantida: 1996).
4. Louie Stokes, *The Tommy Hicks Revival* (Buenos Aires:
n.p., 1954), 15.
5. Excerpt from Gardiner's diary available online at
http://anglicanhistory.org/sa/young1905/09.html
(accessed September 25, 2006).

3 —— A HARVEST OF SURPRISES

1. Gilbert Contreras, interviewed by author April 25,
2005.
2. Miguel Angel Carrillo, interview by author, September
4, 2006.
3. Juan Di Crescienzo, interview by author, 2006.
4. "El Hombre de Galilea Va Pasando, va," public domain.
5. Carlos Annacondia, *Campagna San Martín Mensaje de
Salvación No. 2* (Buenos Aires: El Verbo, 1985), 7.
6. Mara Luciani (assistant to Pastor Zuccarelli),
interview, July 3, 2006.
7. Kathleen Scataglini, e-mail correspondence, May 11,
2005.

5 — Pastoring the Revival

1. Coalo Zamorano, "Jesús, eres mi buen Pastor," © 1998 Grupo CanZion. Used by permission.
2. Guillermo Prein, e-mail, August 6, 2006.
3. Peter Wagner and Pablo Deiros, *The Rising Revival: Firsthand Accounts of the Incredible Argentina Revival* (Ventura, CA: Renew Books, Gospel Light, 1998).
4. Carlos Annacondia, *Campagna San Martín Mensaje de Salvación No. 2* (Buenos Aires: El Verbo, 1985).
5. Claudio Freidzon, *Espíritu Santo, tengo hambre de ti* (Nashville, TN: Editorial Caribe, 1996).
6. Edgardo Muñoz, interview by author, 2006.
7. Ibid.
8. Alfredo Basso, interview by author, 2006.

7 — Keys to Revival

1. Silvia Montemurro, interview by author, July 25, 2006.
2. Pedro Ibarra, interview, June 26, 2006.

8 — Wonders, Gifts, and Miracles

1. Ernesto Nanni, interview by author, July 3, 2006.

9 — Living in Continuous Revival

1. Ricardo Cacabelos, interview by author.
2. Johann Baegert, *Observation in Lower California* (Berkeley, CA: University of California, reprinted 1952).
3. John Shearer, *Old Time Revivals* (Philadelphia, PA: The Million Testaments Campaign, 1932).

10 — What Is God Saying to Us?

1. Elmer Towns and Douglas Porter, *The Ten Greatest Revivals Ever: From Pentecost to the Present* (Ann Arbor, MI: Servant Publications, 2000).
2. David P. Matthews, *I Saw the Welsh Revival* (Pensacola, FL: Christian Life Books, revised edition 2002).